Helping Babies and Toddlers Learn

Helping Babies and Toddlers Learn

A guide to good practice with under-threes

Jennie Lindon

national
children's
bureau

National Children's Bureau

NCB promotes the voices, interests and well-being of all children and young people across every aspect of their lives. As an umbrella body for the children's sector in England and Northern Ireland, we provide essential information on policy, research and best practice for our members and other partners.

NCB aims to:

- challenge disadvantage in childhood
- work with children and young people to ensure they are involved in all matters that affect their lives
- promote multidisciplinary cross-agency partnerships and good practice
- influence government policy through policy development and advocacy
- undertake high quality research and work from an evidence-based perspective
- disseminate information to all those working with children and young people, and to children and young people themselves.

NCB has adopted and works within the UN Convention on the Rights of the Child.

Published by the National Children's Bureau

National Children's Bureau, 8 Wakley Street, London EC1V 7QE
Tel: 020 7843 6000
Website: www.ncb.org.uk
Registered charity number: 258825

NCB works in partnership with Children in Scotland (www.childreninscotland.org.uk) and Children in Wales (www.childreninwales.org.uk).

© National Children's Bureau 2006

Second edition
First edition published by National Early Years Network 2000

ISBN 1 904787 87 8
ISBN 978 1 904787 87 7

British Library Cataloguing in Publication Data
A catalogue record for this book is available from the British Library

Contents

Acknowledgements

My ideas about good practice with very young children have been shaped over the years through conversation with many early years practitioners, advisers and parents. Observation of children has always been key to my approach and has provided vital insights to shift me from an overly adult perspective on what is happening or what seems to be most important.

I am grateful to more people, both very young and grown up, than I can possibly list. However, I would like to express my appreciation to the following individuals who were directly helpful while I was writing this book:

- Peter Elfer, Faculty of Education, University of Surrey Roehampton, Froebel College
- Beverley Hallett, training manager of the Saplings group of nurseries
- Stephanie Moran, early years advisory teacher with the Education Department of Stoke-on-Trent.

Many thanks to the early years teams who made me welcome to sit and watch, and explained how they organise their days with very young children:

- Abacus Nursery, Stoke-on-Trent
- Bridgwater Early Excellence Centre, Bridgwater
- Newtec Nursery, Stratford, East London
- Saplings Nursery, Shortlands, South London
- Staffordshire University Day Nursery, Stoke-on-Trent.
- St Peter's Eaton Square CE Primary School nursery class

Finally, as a parent, I would like to thank Drew and Tanith for being happy for me to quote examples from the diaries I kept of their learning when they were young.

Notes about using this book

Helping Babies and Toddlers Learn includes many examples from my own observations and those ideas shared by early years practitioners. The examples are easy to find as they appear in a box, like this one, and are chosen to illustrate a point or ideas that have been made in the nearby text.

Tinted boxes with a [think] icon mark places where I suggest that you consider a particular issue or choice within the context of your own situation. You may like to reflect as an individual and then, if you work in a team, to discuss your ideas with colleagues.

1. Provision for children under three

There is a broad range of early years provision for children under three in the UK. Different kinds of provision developed because of different ways of working rather than a deliberate intention to vary services. The great variety may seem normal, but it contrasts with the pattern in many other European countries, especially those that have worked to organise a coherent early years service. The UK does not have a publicly funded early childhood service to meet the needs of families prior to statutory education. Different parts of the service are funded in different ways and most of the under-threes provision requires direct payment by parents. In some cases, the fees are subsidised or families can access some form of reduction through tax credits.

We are used to talking about over- and under-threes in the UK, but there are no sound developmental reasons to support the absolute division. The age divide was created because what was called 'care' and 'early education' of very young children developed separately. The early childhood education settings which developed over the twentieth century did not usually take children younger than three years old. (See also the discussion about the care–education split on page 23–24.)

As an introduction to good practice in working with the under-threes, this chapter briefly describes the different kinds of out-of-home provision for very young children across the UK. The availability of these different kinds of provision varies considerably between geographical areas.

Out-of-home provision

Crèches

These groups are informal settings, usually either linked with a facility like a shopping centre or provided as childcare cover for adult activities like meetings, conferences or exercise classes. Some crèches will not take responsibility for very young babies. Children stay in the crèche for a maximum period of time, usually no more than a couple of hours, unless the facility has been set up to cover a conference or training day.

Drop-in sessions and informal groups

This kind of provision developed as a flexible facility for parents and younger children. Parents are usually expected to stay with the children. Such provision may be called a 'parent and toddler group'. Some are still called 'one-o-clock clubs', because they run from that time into the afternoon. Community provision, including the Sure Start programme in England, has often extended the range of drop-in provision.

Different types of full daycare settings

Day nurseries and other types of early years centres offer childcare for parents who need someone else to take full responsibility for their children while they are elsewhere. Parents may be in paid employment or attending a college or university course as students. The different kinds of day nurseries have expanded.

Local authority day nurseries developed for families who had identified social needs. Some settings still offer support to families under stress. However, the development of different kinds of early years centres, including the Children's Centre initiative in England, has blurred many of the previous boundaries around the service.

Provision of childcare through private day nurseries grew significantly through the 1990s. Parents pay fees for full-day places for children from the early months to school age. Some nurseries offer part-time and flexible attendance, some have expanded into care for school-age children. Some nurseries are linked with a specific workplace or college.

Nursery schools and classes

Independent nursery schools sometimes take children from about two-and-a half, though places in state nursery schools or classes are not usually offered to children until they are three years old. Again, provision varies around the country and some nursery schools or classes are involved in developments to become centres offering provision to children between two and three years. Some are also part of local initiatives to work with other local services to provide more hours to families within the day (through 'wraparound' care). The Extended Schools initiative has expanded this kind of provision.

Pre-schools and playgroups

This kind of early years provision traditionally took children between three and five years of age, before they joined primary school. From the 1990s, these groups increasingly lost their five- and then four-year-olds to local nursery or reception classes. Many settings now take two-year-olds and have had to review their care and play provision to meet the needs of these younger children. The facilities usually offer sessional places and operate close to a school term, although some groups have extended into childcare that lasts over more of the day.

At one time, all settings in this category were called playgroups. Those affiliated to the Pre-school Learning Alliance are now known as pre-schools; while other groups continue to be called playgroups, some of which are affiliated to the Playgroup Network.

Home-based care

Childminders

Childminders look after children on a regular, often daily, basis in the minder's own home. In many other European countries this service is called 'family daycare'.

Childminding is usually a private arrangement between the minder and parent who pays for the child's care. Some local authorities employ specialist childminders, for example those who are skilled in supporting children with special needs.

Some childminders are now part of a local childminding network, supported by a local authority development practitioner or adviser.

Nannies

These early years practitioners are carers employed directly by parents to look after children in their own family home. Again, this form of childcare is a private arrangement between families and the nanny. It is the responsibility of the family to make appropriate checks on the nanny.

Developments and changes

Specific guidance has been developed in England and Scotland to describe and support good early years practice for babies and children under three. In England, the *Birth to Three Matters* framework and pack was published by the Department for Education and Skills and Sure Start in November 2002. In Scotland, the guidance provided through *Birth to Three: Supporting our youngest children* was launched through Learning and Teaching Scotland in January 2005. Further resources have followed. Both of these resources were developed to meet the need to guide early years practitioners and make it clear that none of the over-threes early years curriculum frameworks around the UK will simply 'water down' for younger children.

The Scottish and English *Birth to Three* materials look different but have much in common. Each of the development teams took account of the same research base and resources about developmentally appropriate practice for the very youngest children. A further development for England is a birth-to-five framework that should bring together the under-threes and over-threes guidance documents. The aim of this Early Years Foundation Stage is to create coherence between the different documents and to remove the artificial boundaries of 'care' and 'early education'.

The remainder of this book will address the needs of babies and young children themselves and how they can best be supported wherever they spend their days. The ideas you will read about in this book are completely compatible with each *Birth to Three* guidance. In their different ways both the Scottish and English materials focus on how any kind of early years provision – group settings or the childminding service – must be organised so as to:

■ enable babies and young children to develop close, affectionate relationships with their non-family carers

■ value the nurturing of children and respect for their personal care needs, because emotional well-being is top priority for babies and young children – early learning cannot be supported if caring is undervalued

■ understand the holistic nature of child development and that babies and very young children have already started their learning. Good practice for all early years practitioners is to show active respect for children's current interests and preferred ways of learning.

2. How very young children learn

There is no sound reason to make an absolute division between children under and over three in terms of the way they learn or what they learn. However, at the same time it must be remembered that younger children are not just smaller versions of their older counterparts.

Careful observational research supports the wisdom of adults who spend time with young children, showing that babies and toddlers are primed to learn and act upon their immediate environment from the very earliest months. They learn about their world through close contact, including staring and touch. Everything is new to babies, yet within a few months they already have expectations that help them make sense of their world.

Earliest interaction

Since the 1970s, video has allowed us to watch the subtle sequences of give and take that characterise communication between mothers and babies of only a few months old, by using slow motion, freeze frame and comparing timed information from two cameras – one focused on the baby and one on the mother. (For more details of this area of research and the research described on page 11 under the heading 'Other kinds of interaction', see my book *Understanding Child Development*.)

In happy, alert exchanges, the baby was an active partner in this early communication: copying facial expression, learning to pause and look expectant, and reacting to changes in the mother's tone. Babies were aware if their mother's attention was distracted and they made attempts to regain her full attention. There was also evidence that the babies had an understanding of the links between what they did in sound and gesture and their mother's reaction. When babies were shown a video of their mother, they soon changed from happy communication to signs of confusion and distress. The problem was that the video mother's reactions were not attuned to what the baby was communicating and young babies soon became aware of the mismatch.

Early video-based research used mother-and-baby pairs. However, the vital insights about early communication and the sensitivity of babies apply to exchanges between a baby and any involved and caring adult.

How this research can inform your practice

The main lessons for practice to be learned from this research are as follows.

- Even babies of a few months old are keen to communicate. They are responsive to affectionate attention from an adult or older child.
- They are distracted easily and need the full attention of the other person on them for this period of time.
- Equally important, they will give up if their sounds, gestures and imitations fail to raise a response.
- These early exchanges can form the building blocks for later communication fuelled by recognisable words.
- Babies are keen to imitate sounds and facial expressions, and delighted when they are themselves encouraged to take the lead with the adult sometimes copying.
- Babies learn the pattern for interaction – communicate, pause and look expectant, listen to and watch the reply, then make your next contribution.

Infant-directed speech

The video and other observational research projects during the 1970s documented the subtle interplay between mother and baby. Mothers engaged with their babies used a modified form of communication, not the same as with older children, and they followed the young child's lead as well as leading themselves. This form of communication was called 'motherese' by those researchers, a term that arose solely because they did not observe anyone else interacting with babies during the course of their research.

Unfortunately, this term led to assumptions that only mothers, or possibly only women, interacted in this way with very young babies. Further observation in non-laboratory settings easily confirmed that this adjusted form of communication was not the sole preserve of mothers or women, or even of adults. Men, as fathers or early years practitioners, interact in this way with babies. Older children, siblings or interested other children, also learn to talk differently to babies. The children seem to learn through imitation of engaged adults; and their own communicative behaviour is then encouraged by the happy reaction of the babies.

The term 'motherese' has now mainly been replaced by 'infant-directed speech'.

Infant-directed speech used by other children

I have been a happy part of many exchanges characterised by infant-directed speech and those I have observed from a slight distance confirm the great pleasure experienced by both babies and involved adults. Less-experienced practitioners or parents just need to feel confident that this interaction is good for babies and that adults do not look foolish to anyone who understands very young children.

The flexibility of the interaction was brought home to me some years ago when I was in our local café with my own children. My son, then about eight years of age, noticed a rather fractious toddler sitting in a highchair at the next table. The toddler was being ignored by the two adults with her, who were talking to each other.

Of his own initiative, Drew caught the toddler's eye, grinned and then started a conversation with all the qualities of infant-directed speech. His main message, communicated in simple phrases and with lots of pauses and meaningful nods to the toddler, was: 'Life will get tougher, you know. You may think it's hard now. Oh yes you do. But just you wait. I know what I'm talking about. You'll think why wasn't I grateful when I was little? Life was a doddle then', and so on. The toddler moved swiftly from mild interest to full sound and gesture replies, including giggles and chortles, followed by an expectant expression as she waited for Drew to speak again.

Fortunately the adults with the toddler were pleased that she had become happily engaged, rather than annoyed. The whole incident showed not only that older children can be involved in this way with young ones but also that complaining and bored toddlers just want a bit of personal attention.

Using infant-directed speech in your setting

The key features of infant-directed speech are as follows.

- Be close to babies and toddlers, in a way that brings your eyes level with theirs.
- Use ordinary words – there is no need to introduce words like 'biccie' or 'gee gee' – but keep what you say simple and your phrases short.
- Be more expressive than usual speech, both in how you say the words and in your facial expression. Use your eyes, mouth and facial muscles to add to the communication.
- Babies seem to like voices to be slightly higher pitched than normal adult tone. Women start with higher pitched voices, but men comfortable with babies tend to pitch up a little and certainly do not need to strain in order for babies to join in the exchange.
- Good communication with babies has a circling, repetitive quality in which the adult or older child says something similar, not identical, in later circuits of the exchange.
- Infant-directed speech is an exchange, a two-way communication. So pause regularly and look attentive, waiting for the baby's or young toddler's reply. Be attentive and listen to them, whether they have 'real' words yet or not.
- Be ready to follow the baby's lead, in sounds or facial expression. You are partners in this exchange and it is a delight to babies and toddlers when you copy their sounds or expressions.
- Talk more slowly than you would to an older child or adult, but not so slowly as to be tedious or monotonous.

Other kinds of interaction

Careful research into the abilities of very young children has done a lot to challenge the 'everybody knows' clichés about what they can do and how they behave. Children have a great deal to learn but they are making sense of the world as fast as they experience it. Babies and toddlers show evidence of thinking, remembering and acting on their past experience from the earliest months.

Seeing things from other points of view

The received wisdom from theory and a lot of research on under-threes is that they can only understand the world from their own perspective and are unable to take the view of others. This is known as being 'egocentric' – a word which is sometimes misunderstood to mean that young children are selfish, when it is actually just a description of the way that they are beginning to understand the world.

The idea that young children are 'egocentric' in this way is valid up to a point. But the assumption that they are completely unable to see other points of view overlooks the fact that babies, and especially toddlers, are learning very quickly that other people are different from them. Babies do view the world from their own perspective, but there is plenty of evidence that between their first and second birthdays they become able to look at the world from the perspective of another child or an adult, at least for some of the time.

Sometimes, of course, toddlers are utterly focused on what they want, or do not want, and this perspective can lead to some tense moments with their carers. However, life with very young children can be happier when adults not only let the difficult exchange go, but also watch out for signs that toddlers are responsive to how others feel and what they want.

In *How Babies Think*, Alison Gopnik and her co-authors describe a simple experiment in which toddlers begin to show understanding of individual differences. Given a choice between a bowl of raw broccoli spears and cheese-flavoured crackers, all the toddlers chose the crackers. Then the adult showed an enthusiasm for broccoli and a dislike for the crackers, by facial expression and 'yum' or 'yuk' noises. When the adult requested some food by putting out a hand, the 14-month-olds still gave their own favourite of crackers. However, the 18-month-olds fed the adult bits of broccoli, although their expression suggested that they found this a very bizarre choice.

After observing several families, Judy Dunn (1993) saw how toddlers become increasingly aware of how family life operates and of other people's viewpoints, including those of older siblings. It is possible that adults miss the beginnings of this new ability because the evidence can emerge through behaviour that we find problematic. For instance, Dunn reported that by 14 months many younger children could tease and wind up their older siblings. One child, who had just turned two, had learned how to infuriate her older sister by pretending to be her sibling's imaginary friend – a sophisticated piece of thinking, if not a very 'nice' thing to do.

Research into children's developing social behaviour also goes against the cliché of 'egocentric' under-threes. Toddlers show concern for the distress of other children through trying to offer comfort themselves and by directing an adult's attention to the situation. Young toddlers may offer their own teddy or comfort blanket, but by 16 to 18 months, some toddlers offer the comfort object that they know is special to the unhappy child.

Playing together and friendships

Another myth about under-threes is that they do not play together but play 'in parallel', or alongside each other. When discussing this kind of interaction, adults sometimes also say that the children are 'only' or 'just' playing in parallel, as if the children's playfulness has not reached a pattern of behaviour that adults count as real play or playing properly.

Undoubtedly, the playful interactions of babies, toddlers and two-year-olds look different and usually do not last for such sustained time sequences as the play of older children. But plenty of research and observation shows that young children display many of the characteristics of what can only be called 'play', supported by affectionate friendships with other children.

Many interactions can be seen in the visual material collected by Elinor Goldschmied for her Infants at Work and Heuristic Play videos, and in other video/DVD materials suggested in the Resources section. Sometimes, babies and toddlers stare at each other – but sometimes they reach out, become involved in give-and-take and show clear preferences for the company of one child over another.

When you observe young children with an open mind, it becomes impossible to avoid the conclusion that they have friendship preferences and that they really play together.

Perhaps parents and early years practitioners alike are distracted by the fact that under-threes do not always get along and we sometimes have to help resolve the difficulties. However, the idea that there is no real social interaction between toddlers is an adult perspective.

In my experience, a fair proportion of adult meetings and committees include sharp words, disagreements and occasionally somebody physically or mentally removing themselves. Do we then say that the adults are not really working, that genuine work is without disruption or injured feelings?

 ## Games developed by young children

Parents or key persons who observe their young children closely might see many examples of games that are developed by the toddlers themselves, or between siblings. These include the following.

- Communication games of sound-making, giggling, blowing raspberries and nonsense talk are games that may be established between young children and their peers, with older children and with adults.
- Babies and toddlers may lead a game with an adult, such as putting a hand on the page of a book to prevent it being turned and grinning to show that this is a physical and visual joke.

- Alert observers can see subtle games between toddlers when they imitate one another's actions. The games may be actions like head shaking and touching or large movements such as bouncing and leaping off the sofa. Knocking-down activities often absorb children for some time.
- At home, lively games like sofa bouncing or inappropriate use of the video as a postbox may distract adults from observing the playfulness of the exchange, as they might be annoyed that children have created play equipment or materials out of household items. With adult patience

and clear boundaries, children can learn what adults regard as being play equipment and what is not for play.

- When there is an age gap between children, observation soon establishes that familiar games are initiated by the younger as well as the older child and that the younger one creates new versions of a happy shared game.

Watch and listen to the young children in your care.

- Observe and make some brief notes of what children do together, even if the exchanges seem brief, involve no 'proper' toys or sometimes end in tears.
- What has happened during the exchange and does one or more of the children re-establish the game later that day or another day?

What young children's brains can tell us

In recent years, technology has allowed us to establish the nature of a baby's brain at birth and see how it develops over the following months and years. The method is to place a 'geodesic net' – basically a little hat with a large number of sensors – on a baby's or toddler's head. These safe sensors pick up the natural electrical changes in babies' brains when they do something and the messages are then transformed, by a computer, into an image of the areas of the brain that are working.

I am slightly uneasy about whether this research method causes discomfort to babies and young children. (Like any area of new research, we need to be vigilant and ensure that adults' enthusiasm for gaining new information causes no discomfort to the individuals being studied.) But it has clearly established that babies are very far from a blank sheet at birth, although they are not set up with all the electrical connections already made in their brains. The main points that we have now discovered about young children's brains are as follows.

- Babies' brains are poised to go, with masses of potential connections. Experiences, activities, use of their abilities from the earliest days and weeks then contribute to creating actual physical connections within the brain.
- Just because babies have limited physical skills compared with older children does not mean that they or their brains are low on activity.

For instance, they use their eyes a great deal, making an estimated three million eye movements by the time they are four months old.

- Babies and toddlers are keen to extend whatever skills they have as far as they can. Brain research has shown that actual physical connections get made between parts of the brain through babies' activities.

- The desire of very young children to repeat activities and have you 'do it again' is absolutely right for their brain development. Plenty of practice is needed to firm up those electrical connections.

- Babies are active developers of their own brains, so long as they are not restrained from this task by their environment or blockages from adults. A rich complex of connections is made in the very early years, but our brains are not complete for some time to come. Many connections continue to be made and there seems to be another flurry of brain activity and further development in the teenage years.

- Emotions have a chemical effect on the brain. Positive emotions (children being content, interested, relaxed) trigger chemicals in the brain that help make the vital connections. On the other hand, stress and anxiety have a disruptive chemical impact on the brain, blocking the signals.

Using this information in your setting

There are serious implications in this research for how we enable babies and toddlers to learn. Babies and toddlers are primed to learn, but to make the most of this they need plenty of opportunity for early communication, including close physical contact and touching. They need to develop affectionate social relationships, because stress and unpredictability disturb their ability to learn; distressing experiences affect the chemical balance within the brain.

It is crucial that the vast potential for learning in the early years is helped by experiences which are appropriate for a child's stage of development. Potential is lost if parents and other carers relate poorly to babies and toddlers, leaving them insecure or without affection. Their learning is also disrupted if adults overload them or drive them too fast through the necessary stages of exploration and practice. In *Your Child's Growing Mind*, Jane Healy explains the potentially harmful effects of pushing young children on too fast by the visual image of trying to drive a stretch limousine at speed along a forest track. You may be able to make it happen, but it will damage the car and the forest track. You are also likely to create longer-lasting damage that takes time to show.

Young children's brains develop through their active involvement. Adults who over-organise young children are likely to block the vital development of children's own ability to choose and problem-solve; children need to be active learners, following their own interests. So, in many ways, this recent research supports what has been established as good early years practice, that supportive adults:

■ go with the flow of what interests young children at the moment
■ relax with the children and resist any panic-stricken adult agendas to push achievement targets, as this does not bring the children on faster and may well block the very learning that adults are so keen to stimulate.

Encouraging young children's learning in early years settings

In conversations with practitioners and in reading about work with very young children, I have been struck that adults' attitudes towards babies and toddlers are central to how they treat young children, how practitioners decide on their priorities and how they behave towards under-threes.

Good practice depends on a positive outlook on every aspect of the day of a baby, toddler or young child. Here are some simple points to bear in mind that will help practitioners take that positive view.

Under-threes are interesting and valuable now

Practitioners who work with the under-threes are sometimes irritated by the view of colleagues that they have the easier or less interesting part of work with young children. Adults outside early years settings often take the view that 'They're not really interesting until they can talk properly, are they?' or that 'Babies don't do much, do they?'

Planning or recording systems that focus on the major developmental milestones may also overlook the vital fine learning steps that lie between these giant stretches. So much happens in early communication before the first 'real words'. There are exciting successes of balance, wobble and cruising round the furniture before the 'real steps' that start confident walking.

Under-threes are valuable now, for what they can do today, not only for what they will become and be able to do in many months' time. Such a positive perspective is not only important for the well-being of young children. There is inevitably a lot of hard work in caring well for under-threes. Practitioners and parents alike can feel much more satisfied with what they do to care for young children when they realise how much learning is happening at the same time.

Adults who are not geared up to look for early learning may also decide that under-twos and babies are 'a bit boring'. The problem arises because young children tend to be defined in terms of everything they cannot do, rather than what they can. This is known as a 'deficit model of achievement', and is an approach that runs the risk of leading parents or practitioners to overlook (and fail to enjoy) thrilling moments of achievement from the child's point of view.

There are great advantages in challenging this attitude to achievements, and not only for the very youngest children. Older children, who may be thought ready for 'proper learning', are daunted and disheartened by adults who insist on focusing on what they cannot yet do and what they are failing to do right.

Likewise, good practice with children with disabilities is established when the focus is on what they 'can do' or 'can nearly do', and on the individual child's strengths. Children whose physical skills may be hard to achieve will be supported by adults who are excited that Ben can propel himself around the room, rather than wondering sadly if he will ever walk.

Secure emotional and personal development depends on children being able to focus on what they are and can do now. A contented and 'successful' two-year-old in the future will have been allowed to enjoy being the ten-month-old she is today. Such a positive approach is not the same as believing children have to pass through certain stages; it is not that rigid. A positive approach by early years practitioners, and parents for that matter, homes in on babies and toddlers as they are now:

- what they can manage and nearly manage
- what babies find fascinating
- the ways in which toddlers relate to the world around them.

 ## Don't rely on rigid developmental milestones

If you watch very young children, they do not restrict their enthusiasm to what we as adults regard as the major events. For instance, within physical development, we tend to note changes such as crawling or walking. But from a baby or toddler's point of view this milestone is not the final objective they were trying to reach but rather one point on a continuum of movement skills. Once they have managed to do something, their attention swiftly moves to 'now what can I do with this skill?'

Watch babies who have managed to get on all fours but not yet worked out how all the rocking to and fro can be harnessed to move a distance across the floor. Immense effort goes into the rocking, great puzzlement shows on a baby's face when he lifts his head to realise that he is still in the same location. For some babies, annoyance dawns when the greater strength of their arms over their legs means they go backwards before being able to go forwards. The whole point of being able to crawl is that it gets you somewhere and within grabbing distance of interesting objects and people – and the excited look on babies' faces when they finally master the power to crawl tells you that they do not have to have a definite destination; there is immense pleasure in simply crawling around the place.

Watch very young children in your care and work to identify what are the many exciting milestones for them. For instance, your observations may show you that Zainub was thrilled with her first steps – perhaps because everyone clapped – but that a few weeks ago she was equally delighted with her ability to speed-cruise around the nursery. She called out in triumph when she made that first lean across a gap and let go for a moment.

A couple of months earlier she was thrilled to learn how to bounce in time to the music by leaning her hands against the low table and bouncing with her lower half. Who is to say that the first steps were really the most important? Probably not Zainub.

There are positive consequences of noticing and sharing with parents all the fine developments between the milestones. By doing this you show your genuine interest in the child day by day, but there is also less pressure about where and for whom the child performs a few significant milestones.

Caring adults count more than equipment

There has been an explosion in toys marketed for very young children, and commercial glee over research into early brain development. Misrepresentation of that research underpins some aggressive promotion of play materials, electronic toys and video/DVD programmes that are claimed to be vital for early development. However, young children learn from a great variety of play experiences and resources, many of which are neither bought nor are conventional 'toys'.

Parents and early years practitioners are supported by good play materials, but they need to think of themselves as the most vital items of play equipment in the setting. If adults relate fully and appropriately with babies and toddlers, then the children will learn through that relationship; they will feel secure and able to take advantage of the play materials and activities on offer.

If, on the other hand, adults are uninvolved, harsh, neglectful or blatantly uninterested in babies and toddlers, then even excellent play equipment will not make up that loss. Children learn as much from how they are treated by key adults as from what is provided in terms of play materials.

Adults are not the only people important to children. Other children are also vital, both those of the same age and those who are younger or older. In many cases, adults have a central role in enabling young children to enjoy each other's company and learn from each other. Sensitive and caring adults are peace-bringers and mediators, resolving the common daily disputes precisely so that young children can settle back into enjoying each other's company. Just because some playful toddler-exchanges end in a poke or a shove does not mean that they were not playful at the outset and cannot be playful again, once the tears are dried.

Perhaps, as adults, we need to take a few moments to realise this positive aspect once we have managed any distress or arguments between children. Our role as mediator can be wearing (especially on a 'bad' day), so it is important to see how we have helped.

The whole day matters; nurture and personal care matters

Babies and toddlers do not split up their lives into different sections, with some activities regarded as lightweight and others as more significant. Under-threes are ready to learn from every part of their day, and routine activities like physical care matter a great deal to them (see also Chapter 3). Once adults become attuned to the full development of young children, especially to the social and emotional underpinning of all their learning, it becomes so obvious that daily routines matter. They are part of how children feel treated: whether they are valued, or not; and whether they are allowed to have a trusted role in how the day runs.

As an early years practitioner you can look ahead to identify how to use all the learning opportunities and take a baby's or toddler's day as a whole, not as a list of separate activities. It is useful to have plans for each day and young children like some sense of routine. But within an overall framework, it is important for children's well-being that you do not assume some parts of the day are simply routines to be completed in order to reach a more valued part of the day.

Adults who discount personal care time can get very disheartened with the feeling that 'I haven't done anything worthwhile today'. Disheartened adults are less likely to be affectionate companions to young children.

Willingness to look through children's eyes

Supportive and caring adults are willing to make the effort to look through children's eyes, to imagine spending a day in that child's shoes.

- Good observation and communication between adults, as well as with the children, will help you tune into children and acknowledge their perspective, likely priorities and preferences.
- Your own memories can be useful, although adults need to take care that they do not assume the child in front of them is another version of their younger self. However, childhood memories can be valuable in reminding us how much some experiences matter to children, how

warm children feel for being supported and how distressed when their feelings are dismissed or trivialised.

Of course, you cannot know exactly how an individual child feels or thinks about the world, but attentive observation and a willingness to forget adult assumptions will give you a very good start.

3. Quality care is essential for learning

Two distinct traditions developed across the UK in provision for young children. 'Care' settings took responsibility for the youngest children and were originally registered and inspected on a different basis from 'educational' settings. Developments from the end of the twentieth century have blurred these boundaries in terms of what happens within any provision and the process of inspection. Changes within the four nations that comprise the UK have steadily moved towards a more coherent, and sensible, approach that 'care' and 'education' are inseparable in good practice.

There are still some anomalies that persist, most likely because the care–education division within early years provision was never a split between equals. Care was (and by too many people still is) regarded as second best to education, and this tunnel vision has been a serious obstacle in the way of quality provision for very young children. The artificial divide also rests upon professional barriers, such that the more highly regarded, and better paid, professionals (teachers) have tended to work with older children and are more distanced from physical care. One consequence has been that early years practitioners, who are not teachers, have been keen to emphasise their 'educational' role by making statements like 'we do a lot more than just wipe noses and change wet knickers, you know!' In seeking a professional identity, practitioners seem to feel undermined by the qualities of good parenting that are so admired in other social and political debates.

Of course, these adult priorities between care and education make no sense to young children and are swept aside by any informed thinking about children's whole development. If you are a baby, toddler or young child, it matters a great deal how somebody wipes your nose, reacts to your tears or responds when you have wet yourself.

Physical care – that practitioners generously provide and that you increasingly share with a young child who is pleased to be more self-reliant – is central to a contented, well-rounded day. The daily routines of care are not something to hurry through in order to reach those activities that adults call 'educational'. Physical care is an ideal vehicle for a great deal of learning, including warm communication and a sense of self-worth for babies and very young children.

So, babies and toddlers who feel relaxed and who have not been hustled through essential care routines will be far more ready to enjoy everything else that is on offer in your nursery or home.

 ### Tune into children using your own memories of care

Within a team or training group you will have a range of your own childhood experiences to remind you strongly that how you are treated and handled as a child can stay with you as a clear memory. In a group, you might like to express some of these personal insights – without, of course, pushing anyone to share more than they wish. If you work alone, consider your own past experiences.

- Maybe Auntie used to clean your ears with a flannel and then have the cheek to tell you her scrubbing did not hurt.
- Perhaps Grandma used to swoop in from behind with a tissue to wipe your nose without even warning you.
- Perhaps your Mum or Dad was given to ruffling your hair in public, although you said 'don't'.

- Maybe you recall the last time you had a toileting accident as a child and the difference it made if a caring adult acknowledged your embarrassment and helped you find dry underwear. In contrast, how the memory lingers if you were made to feel mucky and stupid.

You will also have adult experiences that highlight the emotional dimension of personal care.

- How do you feel if someone offering intimate services like cutting and styling your hair scarcely talks to you or chats, over your head, with somebody else?
- Many adults have bad health-service experiences of dismissive practitioners who examine you without warning, treat you as a body rather than a person and

talk about you as if you are invisible. Compare those with the positive experiences created by more caring health professionals.

The necessary link to make in discussion, as well as when reflecting on your practice, is that young children also notice the difference between respectful and disrespectful physical care. They also have a sense of bodily dignity that can be affronted, and are left distressed and jangled by being handled without care. Even if they say nothing, their behaviour will show their feelings.

Learning through physical care

Most of the training modules for working with very young children, and a lot of the written material supporting the training, focuses on hygiene, care routines and health risks to babies and toddlers. Care, caring and appropriate hygiene are all important, but the technical side of the routines should be unobtrusive. Of course, inexperienced practitioners need to have the knowledge and confidence to keep babies and toddlers safe from preventable infections, but these skills must be linked properly with a focus on young children as individuals. Hygiene routines should never appear more important than close contact with the child.

Furthermore, safety is not the only aspect to bear in mind when considering good practice in work with young children. I have read sections in books or looked at the caption of an illustration that stresses how young children should never be left alone with food or drink because of the risk of choking. Such a warning is important, but it is equally vital to sit with babies and toddlers because warm attention supports their emotional and social development. Even if an adult claimed to be at a distance that is safe enough to leap in at the first signs of choking, leaving a child to eat without company is still unacceptable. The message to the isolated toddler or child is, 'I have more interesting and important things to do than waste my time sitting with you!' Such adult behaviour is deeply impolite to the child.

Good practice by adults with care routines gives children more than protection from germs or accidents. The experience supports all their learning through the development of early communication and social relationships.

Bringing together care routines and personal contact

Even books which emphasise the idea that babies learn from all their experiences often have separate chapters for care and physical routines, or for baby care. Communication and early learning appears to take a back seat to sterilising bottles, how to feed, how to change and a long list of illnesses and dangers.

Why not look through a range of books for early years practitioners and parents?

■ How far is early learning and affectionate communication still shown within the chapters on how to bottle feed or change a nappy?

■ To what extent is baby care presented as a list of dangers to avoid rather than experiences to promote and enjoy?

Of course, babies and toddlers can be harmed by poorly prepared or reheated milk and food, or they can get serious nappy rash. But, do books or articles give a sense of how time can then be spent with very young children whose carers are protecting them appropriately?

A sense of self-worth

Children who are approached with respect and handled with care will develop a sense of self-respect and feel more at ease with their bodies. Dressing and feeding can support babies because they feel valued. Through affectionate and respectful touch you are showing them 'I care about you as well as care for you'. Babies and toddlers should never, ever feel bundled around like just so much grubby washing.

Babies and toddlers are treated with dignity when you follow these principles:
■ let them know by words and friendly facial expression when you are about to start a feeding or caring routine
■ give them a chance to see and hear you, register your presence and not be scooped up without warning
■ make sure they are ready and know what you are going to do by saying things like 'I think it's time for a nappy change for you' or 'Yes, I know you're hungry, it's all ready, here we go' when you have set up the changing area or lined up the bottle or bowl
■ continue to focus on them and talk gently to them when you feed or change them, in contrast to talking at length with other adults or maintaining a bored silence.

Good practice in offering necessary physical care or help is of continued value for all children. But the importance of establishing good habits and understanding that care matters can be seen especially for children with physical or learning disabilities. They may need considerate and respectful help for months or years longer than their peers. Some children and young people will always need considerable help with intimate physical needs, and genuinely caring routines will be essential for their self-esteem and self-respect.

 How do babies feel?

In her report *How should we care for babies and toddlers?*, Helen Penn asked the intriguing questions: 'What does well-being feel like to a baby?' and 'What is it like to feel good about your body?'

■ What do you think could be the range of answers to these questions?
■ What might we observe in a baby or toddler who felt emotionally comfortable and at ease?

Communication through care

Babies and toddlers will have an extraordinary number of nappy changes, cleaning and feeding times in their young lives, and vital opportunities are lost if these times are seen as tedious chores to be completed as soon as possible.

■ Warm and attentive physical care offers babies and toddlers an experience of personal contact and communication, as well as the sometimes welcome attention to pressing physical needs.
■ Hygienic procedures should be part of a practitioner's confident practice, so the 'rules' of safe practice can fade into the background of the personal exchange.
■ Adult and child are physically close at changing time, so it is an ideal opportunity for an exchange of smiles, or for a conversation of whatever combination of sounds and first words that a baby or toddler can express.
■ As you get to know each child, changing can become an individual experience. Perhaps Donna likes to hear several rounds of 'Ten green bottles' but Harry is a fan of 'Daisy, daisy'. Children will enjoy your personal approach, but your efforts will also help you to feel changing-time is worthwhile.

- Even babies of a few months old will soon show that they recognise the opening sounds and rhythm of a song or rhyme. By three months of age my daughter, Tanith, would grin broadly at my exaggerated opening notes of 'Hello Aunt Jemima' (a music hall song I learned from a day nursery). She would watch and listen intently, and the only way to cut her toenails was with three or four non-stop rounds of the song.
- When babies or toddlers are from a bilingual family, ask if their parent will teach you a song or rhyme from the family language that is unfamiliar to you.
- Babies show personal preferences in how they like to be handled and how vigorously or gently. Perhaps Liam likes to be softly tickled or stroked, Marsha is in favour of energetic arm exercises and Tariq wants to hold onto his favourite toy.

It is perfectly possible to maintain hygienic procedures and still create a personal time. Babies and children show that they appreciate your attention and, of course, ideally this approach should be taken by everyone in a group setting. Otherwise, the likely consequence is the situation described to me at a nursery where there was inconsistency between practitioners. Toddlers voted with their feet and approached the more caring and attentive members of staff when they wanted comfort or realised they needed changing.

There is no way around the fact that there is a lot of physical care involved in working with very young children; it comes with the territory. There will be days when you think a break from nappies and wiping noses would be very attractive. If you focus on how good-quality care supports babies and toddlers, and how you are supporting young children's development just as much as your colleagues with the four-year-olds, you may feel more energised to get through some of the low points.

Shared care with children

A relaxed and individual response to baby and toddler care offers opportunities for children to share in their own care as soon as they are ready. You will notice through observation that even very young children want to take on small parts of the routine for themselves. Perhaps they want to push an arm into a sleeve or to hold their own spoon at mealtime, even if they are not yet adept at getting much food into their mouth.

Toddlers are keen to use their physical skills of coordination in situations that have daily meaning for them. They do not make a sudden move from total dependence to being independent; it is a slow and steady process. The ordinary routines of care are the best vehicle for the very beginnings of self-reliance. You can be pleased about what toddlers manage without pushing them towards a too-early 'independence'.

Equally important, young children experience satisfaction in what they can do and are thrilled that you are just as delighted with their achievements.

Physical contact and genuine child protection

Young children depend upon close physical contact, and parents are criticised if they are distant or emotionally cold with their children. However, some guidance arising from worries about child protection – or misinterpretation of that guidance – runs the risk of creating situations which could be emotionally damaging to young children. Unwise practice is not universal, but some nurseries have established rules like not sitting young children on adults' laps or have set up a witnessing system where more than one person must always be present when a child needs intimate physical care.

Psychologically healthy relationships between young children and caring adults involve close physical contact. The children want to be close and will feel sad and confused if they are kept at a distance. Child protection systems matter, but children are not protected against abusers by such rules and their emotional understanding of affectionate touch and respectful care may be very dangerously affected.

 Valuing care and care routines

If you are part of an early years team or a student on placement, consider and share some ideas about the following. If you work alone, consider your own practice.

- How do you make care an individual experience that helps

very young children to feel valued and secure? What exactly do you do?

- What do you believe currently gets in the way of relaxed routines of changing or feeding? What can you all do to remove any blocks?

If you are a team leader or early years adviser, you might like to reflect on the following:

■ What do you want to see in the behaviour of early years practitioners towards babies, toddlers and very young children?

■ What kinds of support do practitioners need to make the shift if their care is impersonal or rushed? Is the difficulty about attitudes as much as actions?

Learning through the day's routines

The team's outlook is crucial, as is support from more senior team members. Everyone needs to understand how the care routines, approached positively, are an entirely suitable vehicle for learning. There must be no sense of pressure on staff to rush through care routines because, as was explained to me by some uneasy practitioners, 'We've got to do all these educational activities!' These less-confident practitioners had good intentions and wanted to do what they understood to be the best for under-threes. However, they felt pressured by a team leader or adviser who divided 'care' from 'education', or had possibly misunderstood the message.

Teams also need the confidence to explain to others how children learn through daily routines and what their role is in supporting this development. Conversations with parents may be important in sharing a full picture of what young children gain from the day; and can provide an opportunity to invite experiences and ideas from the child's own family. During the first contacts between a nursery or childminder and parents it is important to find out the personal preferences of babies. This not only provides useful and positive information for the babies' later time with you, it communicates clearly to the family that you will take their baby or toddler as an individual.

An assertive approach may be needed to deal with inspectors who apply 'educational tunnel-vision' to slightly older children, even though a great deal of their learning still comes via meaningful routines. One nursery team described their frustration with an Ofsted inspector who left the room at lunchtime before they could stop him, saying that 'nothing would be happening now', so he would take a break. The team used lunch and other routines as meaningful times for counting and number matching. They were most annoyed to find in the report the criticism that the nursery had no early numeracy activities.

 A positive approach to routines in physical care

The key issues for good physical care revolve around the twin themes of positive attitudes and caring behaviour. You might like to reflect on the following points or discuss them with colleagues in a team.

■ Babies and toddlers need a great deal of physical care and some pattern for care routines is important to make sure that their care needs are reliably met. However, the routine should never become more important than the individual children; that is the negative route towards an impersonal institutional pattern.

■ You need to reflect on your existing routines and challenge the bad habits that create non-personal routines, such as group changing time in which every baby and toddler gets a nappy change whether they need it or not. However, it is possible to have a time when young children who have not been changed during a particular part of the day can be checked to see whether or not they need a change.

■ If the physical care schedule undermines a personal touch, perhaps the schedule should be rethought. Of course, it is hard to be relaxed and personal if a practitioner is thinking 'But I've got six babies to get through!' Perhaps the one practitioner should not be changing one baby after another, or the whole team needs to rethink how they value the role of nappy-changing within a day.

■ Likewise, why do babies and toddlers have to take a nap at the same time? They will move towards a pattern that suits adults responsible for a group, but personal care now means flexibility to individual needs.

■ There is nothing inherently positive about completing a care routine quickly or efficiently. Teams need to discuss and reflect on why they value speed. What is the point of trying to be quick? What do we think we will achieve by rushing? Is the price that babies pay really worth it?

This is a small person – not just a body

A rigid changing or feeding time runs the serious risk of adult actions that lose babies as individuals, let alone ruining any chance to support early communication and a sense of trust and self-worth.

In badly run nurseries (and family homes), dangers to babies can arise from careless or unhygienic procedures. However, some of the bad practice anecdotes shared with me by early years advisers or college tutors have highlighted impersonal handling of children and a fundamental lack of caring.

Examples have included adults talking over the top of children's heads at mealtime, pausing only to tell the children to eat up. The clear message to toddlers is that they are uninteresting. Poor-quality practice is led by choices of what is judged to be easier or quicker for the adults, so young children are bundled into clothing because it 'takes too long' to wait for a toddler to add his own contribution of self-care.

One especially queasy description was of a 'conveyer belt' system in which babies were passed along between several adults who each added an element to the changing regime. This staff group had totally lost sight of the fact that a small person came attached to each bottom and that individuals needed attention.

Where adults feel confident to take time over care routines, a sense of positive relaxation develops in the baby and toddler rooms. Emotional warmth and a sense of adults as affectionate resources can be observed in very young children who turn to the adults in distress as well as share enjoyable games with them. Young children show through their behaviour a sense of confidence that they are worthy of care and attention. They expect it to be available when needed and so do not have to demand it through dramatic actions and competing with other young children.

Of course, any baby or toddler room has its fraught moments, but they do not become the main pattern for most days.

The key person system

Quality in work with babies and young children can only be delivered through a caring, personal relationship between baby or child and practitioner. Childminders or nannies within a family home are that key person. In group settings there must be a proper key person system to ensure that an affectionate and personal relationship can develop between individual children, their key person and parent(s).

The main features of this system, when it works properly to support young children are as follows:

- The same, named practitioner is responsible for the physical needs of a very small number of individual babies and toddlers. There is no sense of 'my children' and 'your children'. It is rather that babies and toddlers are given the chance to become familiar with one caring adult in particular and the adult gets to know the child. The key person is responsible for settling a child, responding to their feelings and acknowledging any distress.
- Of course, very young children then get to know the faces and voices of other adults who work in the same room. However, the key person is crucial over the early weeks so that a young child does not feel overwhelmed with newness. Children are the judge of when they are ready to get closer to another practitioner.
- Very young children need to be able to recognise the face of the person who changes them, feeds them or who they first see on waking after a nap. The key person can respond sensitively to individual babies and toddlers, know their preferences and develop personal rituals of songs, smiles and enjoyable 'jokes'.
- Even once young children are settled, it is important that the key-person relationship has real meaning. It works well to have a regular time slot within the day when individual practitioners spend uninterrupted time with their key group of children. Such 'together time' sometimes fits best into 15 minutes before lunch. How the time is spent each day should depend on what children show they would like to do.
- It is equally important for the key person to develop a friendly working relationship with the child's parent(s), who may also be confused by all the new faces of a nursery team. Again, it is not that parents can only talk with the key person, but that there is a familiar face in the early weeks. Parents will then get to know other team members, although the key person will still usually be the one to share the events of the day and communicate important information about the baby's well-being and health.
- The key person will also be responsible for keeping a baby's or young child's records, to track their learning and to make detailed observations. Again, of course, other members of a well-functioning early years team will contribute to the records.

In day nurseries and children's centres it is unlikely that the key person will be working throughout the day. Some settings have a named co-worker, acknowledging that one person will not always be present because of the shift system, holidays and illness. It is important that parents are not then faced with a number of less familiar faces. At least in the early weeks, it is far more comfortable as a parent to know that it will be one of two people to whom you entrust your child at the beginning of the day. You also want to know who will handle the transition back into your care at the end of the day.

Routine, glorious routine

Lunchtime for toddlers in Saplings Nursery

I greatly enjoyed watching and listening to a particular lunchtime in the toddler room at Saplings. The children in this room are aged 18 months to 3 years and take their lunch at half-moon shaped tables where the children have low seats and the adult has a more adult-sized one. The whole atmosphere was one of a relaxed, shared meal that was valued as a social occasion.

- Children helped to dish up for themselves and for each other. I watched one young girl holding a yoghurt carton as another child spooned out what she wanted to add to her mashed apple.
- They poured their own drinks, although adult help was always available if wanted.
- There were few spillages and when it happened, children either fetched the cloth themselves or were reminded, 'It's the yellow one, hanging up over there.' Children were then encouraged to hang the cloth back up again.
- Conversations started, paused as someone ate and then resumed. Between the main course and dessert one girl decided to move across to the other table. The adult on her table simply acknowledged the move with 'Oh, do you want to sit with your friend?'
- Children take a nap after lunch if they want, but one toddler had dozed off before the meal and was being stroked gently as he lay on a floor cushion.
- As lunch finished and the dishes were put on the trolley, a tape of classical music was started as background for rest or quiet activities.

The Saplings' practitioners are well aware of what they are doing and how children learn through daily routines as much as through play. Team discussion, in-house training and a clear philosophy (in this case that of High/Scope) create a situation in which individual practitioners can relax and focus on all the moments with children.

Teatime for babies in Staffordshire University Day Nursery

I sat as part of the afternoon drink and snack time in the baby room. Two older babies who could sit up comfortably were in their low chairs at the table, enjoying oatcakes and drink. One adult sat at the table with them all the time. She was attentive, commented on what was available for tea and what the babies seemed to be enjoying. Far from talking non-stop, she left pauses and some companionable silence.

Part-way through the meal, another practitioner joined the group, cuddling a younger baby who had just awoken. She sat close to the table but in a chair suitable for holding. There was no rush to start feeding the baby who was given a gentle return to wakefulness with soft words and looks. There was a sense of 'welcome back'. When he was ready, then bottle-feeding started but the pair were part of teatime and visible to the babies eating their oatcakes.

The two practitioners sometimes spoke together briefly, but always swiftly returned to looking and smiling at the babies and commenting on what was going on.

Self-reliance and support in St Peter's nursery class

Of course, positive attention and a clear value given to care do not stop with children's third birthday. During an enjoyable morning in St Peter's nursery class, I observed two examples that highlight how genuinely good practice in an early educational setting is vitally grounded in good care. During the morning two girls inadvertently wet themselves. One child was very distressed about the incident and the other was very relaxed about it.

The first child was comforted out in the garden by the team member who was with her. The adult reassured the crying girl by touch and words that gave the message that these things happen, nobody was cross. The child calmed a little and went to change her clothes indoors with the help of another adult. Shortly afterwards, the child became distressed once more. The second team member was equally supportive, giving full attention to the child and reassuring her again. There was no pressure on the child, and the adult waited until she was calmer before continuing with support for changing into dry clothes.

In contrast, the second child informed me (a visitor), 'I've wet myself a bit'. I asked if she wanted any help and she said she was fine. She sat in the corner where spare clothes are stored in drawers with pictures to show what items are available. Bags for the wet clothes are kept in a hanging cloth holder and this child confidently attended to her own needs. Changing her lower clothing probably took 15 to 20 minutes and no adult pressurised her to complete the task. She briefly joined another group at several points in the process, on one occasion chatting with the teacher that she could not find a pair of trousers but thought these leggings would do. The teacher agreed that this was a good idea. Finally, she was re-dressed to her own satisfaction. Smiles, nods and a few words from adults had communicated clearly that the child was doing a good job. There was no move to tidy her up or tuck in her clothes (which would have undermined that message).

4. Learning through close relationships and communication

Children need to form close relationships for their psychological and physical well-being. Their first and enduring attachments will be with their close family and, in many cases, with their mother. But beyond those first attachments children can also thrive in good out-of-home care, as long as their need for close relationships is recognised and a sense of continuity in those attachments determines the way that childcare is organised and given.

Time is needed to form and support attachments, whether within or outside of the family. The close attachment between parent and child is built over months and is not an instant bonding miracle. The consequence is that when young children spend a significant amount of time with other carers, they will form a close attachment to those people (see 'The key person system' on pages 32–34). The flipside is that parents who work or who are students also need to use the time they have with their children to support and develop the family closeness. There are no shortcuts to this and misunderstandings about intensive 'quality time' have misled many parents into thinking relationships can be maintained through very short, concentrated bursts.

Very young children learn best if they are given the chance to develop good personal relationships. They learn through how they are treated, not just by what they see. Experiences of affection, trust and security are all crucial for very young children. Disruptive events and harsh treatment affect children negatively through how they see the world and their expectations, and recent brain research shows that experiences can have a visible and lasting effect on the make-up of the brain well into adulthood.

The three-way relationship: practitioner, parents and child

Elinor Goldschmied (2004) highlighted the essential triangular relationship between practitioner, child and parent. Each part of the shape is equally important, and it is useful to think about the implications of this three-way relationship for your setting.

- Parents already have a close relationship with their baby or toddler. Now they are sharing the child's care with you as an early years practitioner. So they need to feel that your relationship is with their child, but does not cut them out of the triangle.
- You need to form a close relationship with young children, and they benefit from seeing you spend some time in friendly exchange with their parents. Children need to see the link and be helped through transition times at the beginning and end of the day.
- You will be important to young children while they are with you, but their family is their continuity for the future. Their time with you can be special, but should not be separate from the rest of their life.

Do young children demand attention?

Very young children do not hold back from relationships. They do not think 'I shouldn't get too close. I'd better protect myself.' Children are keen to create personal links and be physically close to their key person or minder.

If they are not given the chance to make contact easily, they will try all sorts of strategies to make the contact happen, some of which might be interpreted and labelled by adults as 'demanding' or 'attention-seeking'. Of course children seek attention, it is a natural and positive pattern of behaviour. If attention is easily available and given with kindness, children do not have to 'demand'. This is not to forget that adults often have to share out their time and attention (not to mention that even the most energetic carer gets tired sometimes).

Your aim is not to be perfect (that is impossible), but to aim to give your attention generously, reflecting on the different ways you can show a child that you have noticed: by smiling, touching, using gestures and words.

Children and teenagers who are in the care of local authorities and whose lives have been littered with disruption and rejection, show how destructive it can be if children protect themselves from relationships with others. These looked-after children often resist personal contact on the grounds that there is no point because nothing lasts and they will move on soon. In these circumstances, older children and teenagers whose emotional development has been damaged sometimes take the perspective of not wanting to be 'too attached'.

Shared care means shared affection

When any parent chooses not to spend every waking minute with their children, it is inevitable (and preferable) that the children will form close relationships with the other people who take care of them.

Early years practitioners are often concerned, or feel that parents are anxious, about very young children becoming 'too attached' to nursery practitioners or a childminder. But while parents' feelings must always be taken into consideration, it is the children's needs that should be central. And the children need to form close relationships.

The key person system is sometimes rejected due to a desire to avoid children becoming 'too attached'. I encountered a nursery in which the manager moved the staff around the groups of children every few months because 'the children mustn't get too attached to us'. Yet from babies' and toddlers' point of view, they cannot possibly be 'too attached' to adults who are key in their daily lives. Some under-threes spend many hours in nurseries or with their childminder and they need continuity in these relationships for healthy emotional development.

The idea of being 'too attached' is an adult concept, sometimes used by early years practitioners who are worried about parents' reactions, or who mistakenly think that keeping an emotional distance shows greater professionalism. The phrase is also used by parents who feel uneasy about leaving their child with other carers and perhaps wonder whether that child will get closer to her carer than she is to them.

Adults – practitioners and parents – need to resolve the mixed feelings that exist. Parents who work long hours may well be worried if their young children are clearly fond of their key person or childminder. But these understandable feelings need to be discussed between the adults and not resolved by making it hard for young children to form attachments in out-of-home care. Teams who resist key person systems, or who reject the idea of physical closeness between practitioner and children, often justify their action as helping children avoid the distress of a later parting when they leave nursery, or say that 'it's what the parents want'.

Of course, the situation of shared care is often not an easy one, but problems are not resolved by sidestepping the issue of adult feelings and pretending they have no part to play in the equation; it is not only children's emotions that are involved here.

Shared care means shared affection. However, children's capacity for close emotional attachments is not like a bag of sweets; giving affection to their key person does not mean that children have less for their parents or siblings. Adult problems about 'sharing' a child's affection must not be resolved by organising a nursery, or your home as a childminder, in such a way as to distress children and disrupt their emotional and social development. Even if your intentions are positive, any emotional distance is negative for the children.

Talking and team support

You need to think through and feel through all the issues discussed above and, if you are part of a team, talk them over with colleagues. Considering these matters may not always be comfortable and it may be wise to return to the topic more than once. Team leaders, managers or early years advisers need to help childminders and groups of practitioners consider issues such as the following.

■ In what way can sensitive issues arise when young children form an affectionate relationship with us as early years practitioners? How do we feel and do we have mixed feelings?

- How do we support the child properly and continue to develop the three-way relationship between practitioner, parent and child?
- What kind of support do we want and deserve when we deal with issues around attachment to children and partnership with parents?
- What support would we like when children move on?
- What are the qualities of a warm early years professional? How do we balance caring for the children and caring about the children, as we should, with recognition that we are not their parents?

Emotional support for practitioners

You will notice that, in the box, I use the unusual phrase 'feel through' as well as the more usual 'think through' for issues, decisions and dilemmas in practice. Team managers need to offer support and constructive feedback in helping practitioners to recognise and deal with the feelings they encounter in their work, as well as with the practicalities. Team meetings and supervision sessions should build on opportunities taken to encourage practitioners within the day.

It is no use pretending that early years practitioners do not have feelings and that being a professional somehow means your emotions do not affect reactions and behaviour. Teams need to address issues such as:

- any staff feeling that babies and toddlers should be at home with their mothers, or if there is a sense of 'When I have a family, I won't leave my baby'
- boosting the confidence of less confident, inexperienced or younger staff to present their own skills positively (without support, uneasy practitioners may make themselves feel better by criticising parents)
- isolating any unhappy working relationships with one or two parents so they do not harm other relationships with parents – any difficulties that arise from individual parents must be resolved within that working relationship and stopped promptly from feeding more general claims that parents are 'uninterested' or 'demanding'.

It is very hard to show support and caring for others if you do not feel supported and cared for yourself. Over the years, I have noticed that the nurseries where I observed consistent emotional warmth and commitment given to children have been led by managers who encourage and guide their teams. The manager and senior practitioners have given time and attention when listening to the staff, who in turn feel enabled to give the same to the children and parents. I have known other nurseries where staff have been undermined, criticised and bullied by managers whose only clear ideas have been what they do not want. Under these circumstances, only the most resilient and committed practitioners are able to continue giving wholehearted caring to the children and resist taking their own hurt and frustration out on the parents.

A genuine partnership with parents

A good working relationship with parents is essential because of the importance of continuity in shared care (see pages 32–34). Partnership between parents and carers depends on open and regular communication that acknowledges the contribution of both sides and works hard to avoid any sense of competition. Regular, friendly communication is crucial to ensure continuity – between parents at home and the nursery or the childminder's home – over shared routines and the timing of changes. Babies and toddlers can manage some differences between carers, but not major ones.

Conversation is the best way to keep one another up to date with what a baby or toddler has learned or is nearly ready to do. Ideally, practitioners and parents need to exchange what they notice and to have a shared satisfaction in the baby's or toddler's discoveries and interests.

Warm first contact

Good communication with parents starts from your first contacts, from expressing the same commitment to children and their families as to the practical details about how your setting or service works. It is important to show in a considerate way how you recognise the different attachments that young children make. Perhaps not in so many words, but you need to communicate the following to parents.

- Young children can care very much about more than one person. They are able to make different kinds of close relationships and they can have different special times with a small number of caring adults.

- That they, the parents, will remain the continuity in their child's life. You are pleased to be part of the child's time now, but parents will be there when the child has moved on from your nursery or care as a childminder.
- You are not willing to keep young children at an emotional distance. Explain the sound developmental reasons for this approach. Some parents, struggling with difficult feelings about sharing the care of their child, opt for nursery care in preference to a childminder or nanny, believing that their child will not be allowed to get close. Partnership with parents has never meant agreeing to everything that parents ask you to do and you certainly should not commit to cool, uninvolved behaviour with young children, as if they are their parents' possessions.

Continued regular communication

As the days and weeks roll by, friendly continued communication needs to be much more than giving parents bald facts about whether or not their children ate lunch or requests for more nappies.

- Exchange at least a few words when parents drop off and pick up their children. In the nurseries where I was made welcome, I was struck by the relaxed greetings to parents. A practitioner made the move towards parents and alerted children if they had not noticed their arrival. There was at least a short conversation which included the baby or toddler by words and smiles. There was a full understanding by the teams that, of course you had at least a brief chat with parents to ease the transition time, and not just because something has happened.
- Make it easy for parents to ask about their child's day. Parents, especially mothers, can have an uncomfortable mix of feelings about leaving their children in daycare. They may feel uneasy about asking what their baby or toddler does during the day, what is the usual pattern. Perhaps parents are concerned that the key person or other practitioners will feel put on the spot, that the parent does not trust the practitioners. Your reaction to a parent's comment can make all the difference. A direct approach from you may make it even easier, such as, 'I'm ever so pleased to tell you about Jem's day, you know.'
- Let parents know when babies and toddlers missed them or were happy to see them come back at the end of the day or session.
- It is a delicate balance between reassuring parents that they are not forgotten and avoiding worrying them that their baby cries for ages when they are gone.

- Share what babies and toddlers have done during the day: a trip out, a song or game that was especially enjoyed, a new fine step forwards in the child's development.

- Give parents plenty of space to share with you information about what happens at home, and not just about problems.

- Some parents may feel that trained early years practitioners are more skilled with their children and better equipped to spend the time with them than they are. It is crucial that parents do not feel deskilled in this way. They have many years yet to support their child's learning and it would be a very negative situation if they come to believe they need to hand over to a succession of experts. Some parents may need and welcome help to recognise how much they offer their children through ordinary family life.

- Discussion is important when practitioners and parents share a similar social and cultural background. However, there are different ways of raising children and part of good practice is to step outside your personal experience and childhood, whatever that may be. Early years practitioners need to acknowledge the varied social and ethnic traditions and be honest, as well as keep an open mind, on meeting family needs within the setting.

Be sensitive about significant 'milestones'

It is important not to become too fixed on single developmental milestones, but there is no doubt that parents will feel some events are more important than others. Sensitive nursery teams consider ways of sharing a child's day that avoid, as far as possible, the impression that babies or toddlers are having all their dramatic developmental shifts away from home. This situation is partly addressed by homing in on a wider range of events important to the child (see also page 18).

However, you can also be sensitive by using phrases like 'She's so close to walking, isn't she?' or 'I'm sure he's almost saying recognisable words. Have you spotted any?'

Close relationships with children

You need to develop a warm, personal relationship with each individual child. Babies and very young children do not understand being part of a group; they think and operate as individuals and you have to treat them this way if you are to support their personal development.

The only way to develop a personal relationship with a baby or toddler is to give time and attention from one individual (you) to another (the baby). There are no short cuts.

Your relationship builds up over time, as a young child gets to know your ways and learns to trust in you. You get to know the child, she gets to know you, and you can then help her to make connections.

You need to be physically close to children, and at their level. They are confident that they have your attention when you are quick to sit down with them or gather them in to sit on your lap. As a young child, it is hard to believe any adult is focusing properly on you if that adult's head, and eyes, are far above your head.

It is a matter of courtesy to address young children individually by their own name. Group settings may choose to give the baby or the under-twos room a name, but the children do not think of themselves as 'Daffodils' or 'Green room'.

Young children approach interesting activities or outings as individuals and supportive adults share out their attention, making sure that babies and toddlers do not have to compete with each other. For instance, enjoyable activities like looking at a book or hearing the story read out loud do not work for young children if they are required to sit in a group. A positive attitude towards books, and the best grounding in early literacy, is created by relaxed times with no more than two, or the very most three, young children to share one adult.

Different ways of answering 'what did she do today?'

It is important to avoid the trap of believing that babies must have made something, to prove that their day has been well spent.

Parents can share in what has happened through your words and photographs that you sometimes take.

Many nurseries have a notebook that passes regularly between home and nursery. Some of the content is to communicate practical details about feeding and nappies, and so promote continuity for the child.

The notebook used at Abacus nursery includes a short written section headed 'If I could talk, this is what I would tell my parents about my day.' The record that moves on with the child and finally goes to the family includes a hand and foot print from a child's first and final days in the nursery. There are photos, examples of genuine early art and notes about what the baby likes. Such a record is not only a pleasure for parents, the children enjoy 'my baby book' when they are slightly older.

Children's feelings

Have you heard young children sometimes being told 'You're making a fuss about nothing' or 'It can't be that bad'? The evidence from the child's emotional reaction is that they are not fussing, it *is* something and at the moment it does feel that bad. So what do you think might be going on when adults make that kind of remark?

Babies and toddlers have and express a range of feelings. Adults usually delight in the happier emotions, but often feel uneasy about babies' distress and annoyance. There is a tendency for some adults to claim that very young children do not have feelings or to act as if those emotions are less real than similar feelings in older children.

It can be distressing for adults to see a baby crying in a broken-hearted way, and unhappy toddlers can sometimes be hard to comfort. It is quite usual to see adults, both practitioners and parents, trying to jolly young children out of their distress and to distract them. Adults may mean well but the unfortunate message to the child is that the adult does not appear to have really noticed their distress. Also, children are usually more effectively comforted by the words and physical closeness that tell them 'I know you're unhappy', 'You feel sad sometimes when Daddy leaves' and 'We'll have a cuddle until you feel a bit better'. Speed of recovery is not the main aim for caring adults, but observation and anecdotal evidence suggest that children whose sadder emotions are acknowledged emerge more quickly and with confidence than children who stop in the end because nobody has shown any sign that they recognised the distress.

Learning to understand their own emotions

Even very young children can learn about their own emotions and become aware of the feelings of others. Support for this kind of learning starts with babies and toddlers, and should be given generously to boys and girls. This development is what is meant by the phrase 'emotional literacy', which you may already have encountered. You can help young children with their feelings as much as you support them in their enthusiasm for books and stories that leads later to reading and writing.

- Share in babies' excitement and delight over what they can see or feel.
- But also acknowledge their unhappiness when they show they are sad. Offer them comfort and any practical steps to help in this situation, but avoid any implication that being upset is unacceptable.
- Children whose sadder emotions are acknowledged do not end up as 'cry babies'. When young children feel confidence and a sense of trust that adults are available for the tougher moments of a day, there is no need to make a big drama to get attention.

Realistically, even the most observant adults have to make some considered guesses about the feelings of very young children. Sometimes a child will become distressed or show great anxiety and you could not see it coming. It is important that you do not feel badly if you misinterpret or take a moment to realise a toddler is in a state. Offer comfort as soon as you do realise, and add that experience to your knowledge of this individual child and of how he or she is now more aware of uncomfortable emotions.

Children who receive can give in turn

Adults want children to show kindness and caring to others, to have some understanding of others' feelings, and are quick to criticise the child who is labelled as 'selfish' or 'spiteful'. However, young children have to feel confident that their own needs will be met before they feel secure enough to be generous to their peers, and to develop what is known as 'prosocial' behaviour.

Generous and considerate behaviour develops most easily, and without apparent effort, in those young children who feel cherished and valued for themselves. In nurseries, as much as family homes, young children who easily receive comfort themselves feel able to comfort another young child or to bring an adult's attention to another child who is distressed. In nurseries with a happy atmosphere, the caring actions of the adults are soon reflected in the actions and words of the toddlers and young children to each other – though not all the time of course.

On the other hand, in group settings or family homes where emotional support is thin on the ground, children are far less likely to develop this kind of positive social behaviour. Their competitive and often aggressive behaviour towards each other shows clearly that they know adult attention and care are very limited. Any attention given to another child means there is less for this child – the one who shoves wins. Unfortunately, what often then follows is that the adults interpret this unhappy situation in terms of the children's 'bad' behaviour.

However, adults and their behaviour, or bad behaviour, are as much part of an unpleasant atmosphere as children. Adults under pressure can find themselves well down this particular slippery slope and, of course, some children will bring expectations that everyone fights for attention into your setting from experiences elsewhere. As hard as it may feel, adults need to find ways to steadily move the atmosphere towards more positive exchanges.

Emotions are best supported by people not things

I become uneasy when I hear or read of approaches to children's emotional development that are weighted towards using books and stories, puppets and role play.

All these activities have their place in a well-rounded curriculum for children. However, they are not a substitute for unhurried opportunities for a child to talk with an adult who listens and shows support through words, attentiveness and body language.

If the personal contact is absent or very fleeting, then a story about sadness or sad events is unlikely to help a child who feels great sadness. It is also hard to escape the thought that adults may be using the books and puppets to distance and protect themselves from the child's feelings. It can be hard sometimes to recognise the depth of a child's unhappiness and know that you cannot directly change the source of that distress. But if the child trusts you, you will help through listening and comfort.

Adults need support too

In order to support young children and respond appropriately to their distress, early years practitioners need to feel they can seek support and feel secure and confident about their approach.

A group setting needs to establish a clear model that children's feelings will be acknowledged, practitioners will not try to jolly children out of distress and children's feelings will never be belittled or denied.

Inexperienced practitioners may need guidance from the manager or more experienced members of the team that good practice means responding to the emotions that children express, not avoiding them. The less experienced and the younger practitioners may also need individual support, through supervision, to deal constructively with their concerns about children's distress.

Practitioners need to feel confident in their turn that having a crying baby or toddler in their room will not lead to criticism of their skills or be seen as a failure on their part. Failure would be ignoring the child.

The early years team in a group setting must discuss genuine professionalism and ensure that the message is communicated to, and understood by, everyone on the team. Good early years professionals are not distant from children's feelings, nor are they without feelings themselves. Of course, nursery practitioners, just like nannies and childminders, need to find a close relationship with children that is different from, and supportive of, parents' attachments.

Children's relationships with each other

While it is crucial to look at how adults relate to young children, it is important to recognise how much even young children can mean to each other. In the UK we have highlighted the significance of adults for children's development, and it is time to reflect whether this well-intentioned emphasis has gone too far in the other direction. The risk of an imbalance is the implication that adults are the only important people in young children's lives.

Helen Penn (1999) describes the Loczy method, developed in Hungary. This approach recognises that children need to maintain autonomy, so focuses on reducing the level of adult intervention and potential interference. It shows great awareness that other children can manage their own and each other's play; they do not always need adults to be directly involved. Penn also points to the explicit aim in the Reggio Emilia nurseries in Northern Italy to foster a collective feeling between children and adults. Furthermore, many Danish nurseries bring the age groups together and encourage the slightly older children, especially siblings, to nurture younger ones. The assumption is that care-giving is not the sole territory of adults.

Good practice with children and families means that we are all willing to reflect on what we do and why. People who work with children are often on the receiving end of quite enough criticism. So it is important to stress that saying we might have over-emphasised the adult role absolutely does not mean that current practice is all wrong.

It is a question of balance. Nurseries I have visited who focus on what the children do together have often simply re-established the importance of relaxed observation skills, of looking and listening to what very young children do with each other and seeing the value of their interaction, rather than believing that most or all valuable input comes from grown ups.

Promoting young friendships

You can help children to make friends and play with one another. There is a persistent myth that young children do not make contact and only play alongside each other (see page 12). However, if you watch carefully, you will notice that babies do make social contact within the limits of their physical skills, and toddlers often develop games together. Young children form friendships and can be caring towards each other. Adults can acknowledge and support this development in different ways.

- Be ready to watch children and notice how they make contact with each other.
- Acknowledge with the babies and toddlers that you have recognised their social gestures, for instance by saying, 'Yes, Danny's here! Are you

going to join him?' to a baby who is keen to crawl across to a newly arrived child.

- Be tolerant if the contact moves of very young children look a bit 'clumsy' or likely to hurt. You can help pokes to become touches and look at toddlers' faces to check whether the full body hug of their friend is welcome or not. Look first, rather than move in too fast with the conviction that they will hurt each other.
- Avoid telling children that another child is 'your friend'. Watch for the signs through words and actions that support this conclusion.

Children cannot possibly make friends unless they have enough time together and can reasonably expect to see each other in a nursery, a drop-in or a childminder's home. The pressure for parents' choice and high flexibility in childcare appears in some cases to create situations in nurseries and playgroups where children attend on highly variable patterns. This flexibility may suit families, and nurseries may reasonably say that they are responding to demand. However, from the children's point of view, they may see different children's faces each time and so the experience loses the social value for them.

Reflection on this issue does not mean that some flexibility of service is wrong; it means that children's experience should be properly considered as a factor in quality of service.

Promoting contact between children of different ages

Children in family homes are not kept in firm age bandings; siblings mix with each other. However, any nursery with a wide age range has had to address the question of how to organise smaller and more manageable groups of children. Over the years, day nurseries have experienced different organisational patterns and there is probably not an absolutely right system.

When I first worked with nurseries in the 1970s, they had recently moved from age-grouped rooms to mixed ages, known then as family grouping. The aim was to provide children with contact across the ages, but gearing activities to the very different needs of a wide age range posed some practical problems. Several nurseries that I visited created the necessary flexibility by having times of the day and week when children enjoyed activities within a narrower age band.

I recall listening with great interest to a thoughtful team in one north London day nursery in the late 1970s. They had re-established a baby room, what became known as the 'pre-school room' for three- to five-year-olds, and the middle band was for mobile toddlers and two-year-olds. The two practitioners in this middle-band room had noticed how much they needed to adjust the activities, including arts and crafts, that had regularly been available in the family groups. This reflection had made them consider that the 18-month-olds to rising threes had not been as well supported as possible in the previous arrangement. These young children had managed, and had not been treated inappropriately as babies. However, a room dedicated to their age had shown that they approached play materials and activities in ways that were different to the three- and four-year-olds.

The return to age grouping seems to have been in response to the practical concerns mentioned above, but they also make it possible to meet the different ratios required by national standards. The downside of firm age grouping is that babies and toddlers lose the opportunities to learn from the older ones. However, slightly older children relish contact with younger ones and often flourish with the opportunity to show caring and to help. I have observed different ways of supporting this kind of contact in nurseries with different spaces. Some examples appear in the box above.

Organising a setting to help promote relationships

Bridgwater Early Excellence Centre

This combined children's centre has large rooms with different areas. In one room, the babies and toddlers have their own section, at the back of which is a quiet room for rest and peaceful activities, like using the Treasure Basket (see page 66–67). This area which is specially for babies and toddlers is divided by a low internal picket fence, with a gate.

Older children are welcome to enter the area and make friendly contact with the babies. However, activities are kept peaceable here, so there is no risk that crawling or uncertainly mobile toddlers will be knocked over by enthusiastic four-year-olds. The smaller items of play equipment are also kept on the other side of the picket fence.

On the day of my visit, the babies and toddlers showed interest and a wish for contact with those older children who chose to join them. A play-dough activity on a table was enjoyed by the older children and watched with fascination by the younger ones. A couple of four-year-olds helped in the care of a baby and offered her toys, with an adult close by.

Staffordshire University Day Nursery

In this nursery the younger children start and end the day with the older ones, although the babies and toddlers each have their own room and staff. Not all children stay for the full day-nursery hours, so numbers are lower at the beginning and ends of the day. However, the age mixing is not simply a practical step; the team see the value of enabling the different ages to spend time together.

I spent part of the afternoon with the nursery and saw how the babies enjoyed their snack time (see the example on page 35) and then moved with the babies to join the toddler room. The babies were in their appropriate seats so they could see what was happening and they looked with interest. Toddlers made friendly contact by look and touch and the adults watched, reminding the toddlers not to give the smaller toys to the babies.

By the last hour or so of the day, the babies had left for home with their parents, and the toddlers who remained joined the room belonging to the three- to five-year-olds. The practitioner responsible for this room had a chat with the older children to encourage them to consider what to lay out on the tables, reminding them that it would not be wise to pick anything with little pieces. The toddlers joined the room, showing interest in what was available and settling down in their chosen part of the area.

Abacus Nursery

The team provides regular opportunities for older siblings to visit their baby or toddler brothers and sisters. Other children also visit and spend a little time with the younger ones, accompanied by an adult.

Newtec Nursery

The team encourage the older children to move about the nursery and visit the baby room on errands. The children enjoy being trusted to take a message to the staff of the baby room. A verbal message is often supported by a written note that, again, the child feels has been entrusted to them to hand over to another practitioner. The older children are also given the responsibility to take and bring the register for the baby room.

The Newtec team also recognised how much the older children, some of whom have been with the nursery since they were babies, like to have access sometimes to the materials made available for the younger ones. There are times when a selection of 'baby toys' or equipment, such as the canvas tunnel, is brought in to the main room. Children enjoy playing with the materials, as well as the chance to be very young for a while.

Communication

Positive relationships with young children are completely interlinked with warm and developmentally appropriate communication between adults and children. Early communication underpins the extraordinary task achieved by most children, that of learning to talk.

There are a number of complex theories that try to explain how very young children all around the world learn the fully formed language that they hear from fluent speakers. In many societies and communities, these very young children learn two or more different languages. No theory has a full explanation of how children manage this task. Each theory can potentially explain some of what happens, but then falls apart in attempts to explain and predict other aspects.

Grand theories are of less use to practitioners and parents than observational research and records of young children's early spoken language. This kind of material, along with observations made by adults involved with children day by day, has shown that children's early communication is firmly grounded in affectionate relationships. We can still speculate on how young children manage such an obviously difficult task, and part of the answer seems to be that they are ready-wired in the brain to take on language.

However, the building blocks to full communication are much more social than technical, and the best guidance for adults to support this development is actually very straightforward.

Social communication

Young children do not only learn the words and grammar of spoken language, they also learn its social uses and context. There are opportunities for full communication with young children throughout the day, and talking with children should never be seen as something you do when you finally reach a designated playtime.

- Make sure you spend plenty of time close to babies and toddlers. Young children do not communicate over a distance; they need to be sure that you are talking with or listening to them as individuals. (See also the section on infant-directed speech on pages 8–10.)

■ Be guided by the timing that suits babies and toddlers. Communication with very young children cannot flow if adults are driving it at speed. There has to be a sense of relaxation and shared enjoyment. Babies do not benefit from being talked at, any more than older children.

■ The key point is to listen and look, as well as to talk yourself to babies and toddlers. Children do not learn through being drowned in talk, even when well-intentioned adults are convinced that their words and phrases are definitely 'educational'.

■ Follow the children's own lead at least as often as you start a game or direct their attention to something interesting. Your shared focus might be their favourite pudding, building a brick tower, catching sight of the squirrel in the garden or a toddler's clear request for a favourite song or rhyme with hand movements.

■ Watch out for children's full communication. Before they are able to attract your attention with words, babies will use eye pointing, gestures and hand pointing. You can support the development of their communication by responding fully to these messages. There will always be some uncertainty, but you can acknowledge this with words like, 'Is that what you want?' or 'I'm not getting this, am I? Let's go closer and you can show me again.'

■ Avoid absolutely, the brightly coloured consoles that claim to 'teach your child to talk'. Children do not learn language from pressing buttons with pictures and then hearing a disembodied voice say a word. Fun with sounds, early conversation and learning the names of objects and people happens within the context of social interaction between children and adults, and between children themselves.

■ Language is a social ability and children learn to speak from real people, not from hours at a screen – either a computer or the television. Television and video can be a valuable activity, so long as it is used selectively and enjoyed with the child. Young children may comment on what they see and hear at the time, or perhaps remember afterwards. Used well, television can be an active, not a passive, experience for young children.

Boys and girls

It is crucial always to be mindful of ensuring that you communicate as fully with young boys as with girls. Observational evidence supports the claim that children are treated differently on the basis of their sex from an early age, even by adults who are sure that they treat all children alike.

In some ways, this aspect of good practice is a reminder that fair treatment often involves treating children slightly differently. For instance, early years practitioners are overwhelmingly female, and it is very easy to believe that girls want to have more conversations if you do not tune into the boys' interests. Children pick up on subtle clues to adult disinterest or the sense that adults believe some other focus is more important than what absorbs you as a boy.

In a similar pattern, there are some signs from observation of adults that they are more forthcoming in acknowledging and talking around feelings with girls than boys. The boys pick up the message that feelings are not for them, or not to be voiced, and then the adults say that the boys do not want to communicate about emotions.

Talking with young children who do not yet talk back

During the time I was writing this book, I overheard a lovely exchange between a parent and toddler that floated over from the next cubicle in my local swimming pool.

The parent was remarking on events for the toddler with comments like, 'That's my swimming costume and that's yours' and 'Right, I've got my costume on, now it's your turn'. The switch to the toddler was signalled with 'Let's get your vest off', 'Well done' and 'Now put it in the bag', and the toddler echoed '...in the bag'. Then there were sounds of mild complaint from the toddler and the parent's voice continued, calmly and gently,

'No, sweetheart, your costume goes on you, not in the bag'. Further toddler complaints were met with low-key words including the deal of 'Okay, I'll swop you' and then 'Well done, you look lovely'. Then parent and toddler emerged ready to negotiate the lockers, followed by the pool.

I could hear from the parent's voice all the time that this was Dad, not Mum. The example is a good reminder that neither mothers, nor women, have cornered the market in patience, a calm approach and a willingness to compromise. Here was a man who felt comfortable with the kind of low-key commentary that helps toddlers to feel at ease with the events of the moment. His daughter was also enabled to hear spoken language in a meaningful context from an adult who adjusted to what the toddler communicated at each new moment.

Many of the qualities of helpful communication with young children, who have words, are the same as the good habits adults need to develop in supporting communication before spoken language emerges. Further issues that emerge include a sensitivity to our own adult communication habits and willingness to reflect and exchange constructive feedback with colleagues.

The use of questions

Adults need to hold onto those qualities of good communication that enable children to be equal partners (see above), once children are able to talk. An adult concern about 'getting them to learn' can lead to unhelpful habits.

It is important that adults listen as well as talk. Useful adult questions for a child's learning are open-ended and encourage further exploration. Yet it does not help children when adults develop a habit of overusing questions, even sometimes replying to a child's question with another question. Sometimes children just need you to share information directly. Adults' use of questions needs to be thoughtful and not weighted towards 'testing' questions, those for which the adult knows the answer.

Questions about questions

In Saplings nursery, the team consider the helpfulness of questions that adults ask children and use a guideline of reflective questions for themselves:

- Is the question you are asking the child a genuine question?
- Do you really want to know the answer?
- Does the child have the answer and you do not?
- Would you ask an adult this question?

Disabilities that affect communication

Some young children will have disabilities that affect communication. Physical disabilities may influence how a child is able to make sounds or communicate clear messages through gestures, facial expression and body language. Learning disabilities may influence the pattern of development, and connections between an experience and how it is named and described.

Children with disabilities affecting communication may need further specialist help, but the good habits needed by adults in early communication provide a very positive framework. Children are supported by an adult outlook that considers full communication and looks for the ways in which this individual child indicates interest and enthusiasm as well as dislike or resistance. The willingness to use non-verbal as well as verbal forms of communication, and readiness to repeat in different ways, will help a child who is simply going to take longer to learn. Some young children will benefit from more than your generosity with gestures and need communication through a signing system. Simple visuals can ease communication for some children.

As many settings become more inclusive, early years teams need to be aware of the possible impact of disabilities on young children's experience and needs. However, appropriate adjustments to communication should neither overlook nor lose sight of the personal and developmental needs that disabled children share in common with their peers.

5. The importance of physical skills

The thrill of physical control and exploration

If you watch young babies it becomes clear how keen they are to use their current physical skills to the utmost. In the early weeks and months their physical control extends from the head downwards and from the central line of their body outwards to their limbs. Given space and safety to practise, babies put great effort into abilities such as trying to hold up their head, grasping and bringing objects towards them, moving themselves about and using their growing skills of coordination to act upon the people and objects in their environment.

Babies and toddlers need to practise their skills many times, and helpful adults not only enable them to enjoy this repetitive fine-tuning but show their own pleasure in what very young children can now manage. Older children on the climbing frame will sometimes ask for help, but much more often they say 'Watch me!' Babies and toddlers give the same message through eye contact, grins and performing fancy physical movements many times.

Mobility is a serious issue for babies and toddlers. Until they can move themselves from one location to another, they are dependent on adults or older children to move them to somewhere interesting or bring the interest to them. Left to their own choices, babies and toddlers assign a great deal of time and energy to getting on the move and using the physical skills that are already within their control.

Within the first year of life, babies apply their skills in different ways to further their drive for exploration. They are still learning how the world works and so, to adult eyes, babies and later toddlers use their skills in an indiscriminate way. From the baby's point of view, feeling, exploring and watching is key; they do not have the knowledge to consider whether they should grasp or touch something. It is an adult responsibility to keep them safe without unduly restricting the exploration. Of course you are concerned about danger; you do not want young children to hurt themselves. But it is very useful to recall that toddlers are not deliberately putting themselves at risk; they have much to learn.

The need to move

The most recent research into brain development (see pages 14–15) shows that the way in which babies and young children use their body is important for their attention and concentration. They need to move around their environment using all their senses. Vital feedback is gained from experiencing movement, balance and the hands-on kind of play and learning that has been emphasised for so long in good early years practice.

An important lesson from brain research is that children need to use their current skills and not be pushed prematurely into skills that adults feel are somehow more appropriate, such as sitting up and playing with table-top play activities. Most practitioners would probably be sceptical of attempts to make babies walk before they are ready, but they might not question the idea of sitting infants in such a way as to keep them still and restrict their natural desire to move and explore. Babies and toddlers can, and do, concentrate perfectly well on the move and at the various stopping points that intrigue them as they move from place to place within a familiar environment.

Staying still is hardest of all

A child does not need to stay still in order to concentrate. In fact, attention to what their body is doing is a vital part of toddlers' growing confidence in their movement, as Sally Goddard Blythe (2004) shows.

The ability to stay still is the most mature stage of the movement skills. If you watch a toddler or young child in the early stages of any of the large movements, you will notice that getting up some momentum is a vital part of keeping balance. Toddlers who stop in their walking often sway a little and plop back down on their bottom before getting up and trying again. Even older children, such as those learning to ride a two-wheeler bike, realise that riding very slowly is hardest of all. You may recall (I certainly do) the scary moment, as an inexperienced bike rider, when you have to get yourself from no movement to enough forward momentum to feel properly secure.

The most advanced level of physical movement in children's development is the ability to stay completely still. So, it is scarcely surprising that young children do not relate well to lengthy group activities that require them to sit quietly and listen or look. They are not being naughty when they squirm about and then disrupt each other and the activity. Yet sometimes adults will say the failure of this group activity shows that the children 'cannot concentrate'. On the contrary, the children are probably fully able to concentrate, if they are allowed to use their physical skills and directly experience materials. They just cannot concentrate yet in this way; the requirement to be still is actually the source of the disruption to their powers of concentration.

If you find you and your colleagues are experiencing this kind of frustration, reflect a little on what you intend the children to learn through this sit-down activity that is not working for anyone. Think creatively about other ways, and other parts of your setting, that could promote this skill or area of learning. Consider especially ways to learn 'on the move', and you will probably find that both the children and you experience a more satisfying time.

Physical experience builds towards cognitive skills

Toddlers and very young children should be allowed and encouraged to practise and fully explore their larger movements. They need confidence in the larger muscle movements before they are able to manage the finer ones. It seems very likely that trying to fast-track children through the less valued physical parts of development towards the more valued cognitive learning tasks is actually counter-productive – quite apart from the fact that this so often creates frustrated and confused toddlers.

■ Children who have not been allowed to move about a great deal will not be ready to be still.

- Children who have not stoked up plenty of experience of balance and use of large movements will not be able to make the fine movements and controlled eye movements that are vital for reading and writing.

Toddlers need space to move, and relish adults who enjoy physical games with them. Plenty of crawling gives babies direct experience in head control and the independent use of the front and back of their bodies that is clearly such a tough task at the beginning of crawling. This movement helps a baby to synchronise their balance with a steady frame created by hands and knees in contact with the ground. They also synchronise movement and vision within an activity that sends vital messages to their brain about what it feels like to be in balance, to have your balance feel rather wobbly and to lose it altogether.

Older toddlers still love to creep and play crawling-chasing, and wriggle forward on their stomachs, even when they are confident walkers. They have experienced sufficient activity to be confident in how it feels to move their body deliberately, to create forward or backward momentum and to stop out of choice, rather than because they have crashed into something.

Many early years practitioners are concerned about pushing three- and four-year-olds towards ever-earlier pencil control and paper work at the table. The most recent research, including that on brain development, supports their concern. Many young children are not yet ready for this level of fine movement and coordination, especially under the atmosphere of anxiety that sometimes accompanies the activity. All too often I have heard from practitioners about children who sadly say that the least enjoyable part of nursery is 'having to do my work'.

Physical activities and space to move are immensely valuable in their own right for children's development. It is not simply the case that young children need to let off steam. Creative thinking about the use of the outdoors is reminding early years teams how much young children can learn out in the garden or on local trips, and how much they enjoy this time.

I have heard and read encouraging anecdotes about sensitive teachers in the early years of primary school, who are recognising the futility of long periods of sitting for five-, six- and seven-year-olds. I hear of regular breaks for an indoor stretch, a brisk 'power walk' for everyone around the playground or an enjoyable run about for adults as well.

The shift to physical action and some fresh air bring mental refreshment and a greater ability to get back to classroom-based activities and really focus.

 Toddlers as entertainers – deliberate use of physical skills

Toddlers show their sophisticated bodily awareness through visual jokes based on movement. Watch the toddlers in your setting and see what you can observe. I have noticed examples like the following.

- Games with an adult or another child that involve give and take and give again. Toddlers delight in their confident control of their movement and its application to a joke game.

- Collapsing or falling over deliberately, sometimes many times if this action raises a laugh from adults or older children.
- Experimenting with actions that they recognise as unusual, like trying to walk backwards or enjoying the game of being walked around by their feet resting on those of an adult.
- Teasing, often of an adult, by going close to something that is 'out of bounds' and then backing off a little, all the time watching for the adult's reaction.

Learning through exploratory play

If you watch babies you will see that they have a favourite method of exploration for the moment, and that this approach is applied to any interesting objects within range. There is not a rigid pattern but you can observe the unfolding of the following methods of physical exploration.

- Holding something is interesting in itself when babies have managed the coordination of looking, reaching and grasping.
- Babies put objects in their mouth on a regular basis, and toddlers still use the sensations of their lips, mouth and tongue. In the first year of life, babies experience their clearest sensations through their mouth. So, although adults need to keep an eye on hygiene and safety, babies are taking the fast track to learning.
- Once babies can hold onto an object with confidence, they inspect it, often with attention to minute detail. Within their physical skills, they will often turn the object to look from a different angle.

- Babies become intrigued by doing something to an object or person. They experiment with patting, hitting, poking or pushing.
- Objects that can be held securely are sometimes shaken. The action may be repeated if something interesting happens, such as a noise.
- Once two hands can be coordinated, babies often examine objects in great detail, turning them about and upside down.
- The ability to hold something and move two hands in different directions gives babies the opportunity to find out that some things, like magazines and other paper, can be torn, with a satisfying sound and effect.
- Some babies become intrigued by the feel of objects against their face and gently rub a toy or other object against their cheek.
- Babies who can grasp and hold something do not immediately work out how to let go again. Once they manage the skills of release as well as grasp, babies can become enthusiastic about dropping or throwing objects. Of course, they have no idea initially about appropriate objects for dropping and throwing. It is fair that adults help them learn the distinction, while understanding the value for babies of this activity.

The first birthday does not bring a dramatic change. Toddlers still use many of their favourite methods of exploration, but some approaches fade away or re-emerge in new forms. These might include the following.

- Dropping objects is still of interest but is now often combined with dropping through something, perhaps posting an object through the banisters in a family home.
- Holding, stroking and rubbing objects can be fascinating to toddlers but this physical action is used in a more deliberate way, perhaps with soft materials or textured surfaces.
- Toddlers have the skills and understanding of their environment to relate two or more objects to each other in deliberate ways, both imitating the actions of others and also in creative, new approaches that are their own invention.
- Young children have a growing understanding that some objects have special uses and they sometimes use their knowledge to make a visual joke, for instance that a bowl is used temporarily as a hat. The physical action is also intriguing evidence of the thinking powers of toddlers, since the humour depends on the interaction of 'you know that I know that you know that this is a silly thing to do'.

- If you watch toddlers you also see how much they like to organise and move objects around, so they need plenty of materials that can be treated separately. I call this kind of toddler activity 'piling and filing'. Young children relish putting one object into or on top of another, sorting out an array of objects in ways that make sense to them, reorganising them and putting them in and out of larger containers.

The frustration of the toddler-scientist

Toddlers also learn, sometimes to their temporary sorrow, that some actions of immense scientific interest and dramatic effect are unacceptable to adults.

Some years ago I watched as the young son of close friends very carefully tipped his yoghurt over the head of the family dog who was sitting by his high chair. The impact of falling yoghurt on a dog's head was fascinating: a kind of splat and spread effect. The dog, although initially surprised, appeared to like the taste of the yoghurt. The toddler's parents, understandably, were not pleased and made it very clear that yoghurt was not to be used in this way. Their son looked disappointed but took the point.

Respect for children's schemas

As well as the physical actions themselves, you can observe regular and deliberate patterns in how individual toddlers act upon interesting objects in their environment. Chris Athey developed the idea of schemas, from Jean Piaget's approach to the development of young children. Cath Arnold (2003) clearly describes this, outlining how very young children often choose to explore around a theme. For instance, they might spend some time over days exploring ways to enclose or wrap objects (an 'enclosing' schema), finding out how to move objects from place to place (a 'transporting' schema) or trying out creative ways to physically connect objects together (a 'connecting' schema).

Toddlers do not, of course, devote all their energy in their exploratory play to their schema of the moment. However, observation can highlight these connected themes and is an important part of looking through toddlers' eyes. Play can just look like 'making a mess' or 'getting into things they shouldn't' until adults stand back and really watch the planned and experimental nature of some play. Of course, adults are responsible for keeping children safe and establishing some boundaries for what is transported, connected or enclosed.

You will notice that children between two and three years old still follow individual patterns of interest and enjoy the sheer sensation of some materials. Their impressive array of physical skills and a broader understanding of their world can now support deliberate exploration and experimentation to see 'what happens if...'. Toddlers who have been enabled to concentrate in their own way when younger are becoming young children whose behaviour looks more like 'proper concentration' to inexperienced adults.

Two- and three-year-olds often persevere in relatively long sequences of working out what can be done with the given materials, trying different methods if their first choice is unsuccessful in their terms. Toddlers sometimes work separately, but it is possible to see how focused two- and three-year-olds, who know each other, work cooperatively on a shared task. By words and gestures, they often divide up simple sub-tasks in how they move the dirt around in the garden, build something out of sand or transport bricks from one side of the room to the other.

Resources for exploratory play

Elinor Goldschmied gathered many observations of the exploratory play of babies and toddlers in their own homes and from time spent in both English and Italian day nurseries. She noticed that children were continually fascinated by ordinary objects: the delight of saucepans and a wooden spoon. Goldschmied was concerned about the loss of such natural materials and of meaning for children when adults felt pressurised to push children into the learning that was supposed to be achieved with bought toys and play equipment. She has promoted materials that support all children's five senses, but has also focused on the importance of what she called the 'sixth sense': children's sensitivity to their own bodily movement and recognition of what the many physical skills feel like to the child.

The treasure basket

This resource is intended for babies once they can sit comfortably with support, and remains a valuable source of exploration for young toddlers. The idea is to

gather a range of materials that vary in feel and texture and keep them in a
low, open basket. The aim is to avoid any commercially made toys and plastic,
since this material is so dominant in bought play materials.

You collect ordinary objects that are safe for babies to handle, including
putting in their mouth. You may have small containers, large cotton reels, fir
cones, woolly balls, a firm fruit like a lemon, a wooden spoon or spatula, large
wooden curtain rings, a bath sponge, a small scoop or pastry cutters or the
larger type of wooden clothes peg.

There are no firm rules for the contents of a Treasure Basket except that the
material can be wiped clean and nothing is so small that babies or toddlers
could swallow it. (If you use the Treasure Basket resource with older children
with learning disabilities, watch out for size since they will get larger objects
into their mouth.)

The collection should vary in look, texture, shape and smell so that babies can
explore in any way they wish. The idea is that an adult is close by but allows the
baby, or two babies sitting on either side, to explore the materials in whatever
way they like. There is no need to comment on what the babies are doing, nor
to intervene unless there is a genuine safety issue. Just sit close and enjoy
watching.

Heuristic play

Elinor Goldschmied worked collaboratively with Anita Hughes (2006) and
Gwen Macmichael to develop the idea of the Treasure Basket into special play
sessions that were introduced into day nurseries, although a similar resource
works equally well in family homes. She called the activity Heuristic Play, from
the Greek word *eurisko*, meaning 'gain an understanding of'.

For a nursery, you need to gather a wide range of materials so that there
will be more than enough for a small group of toddlers. A similar resource for
home use could be one large bag or box of materials. The materials are similar
to the Treasure Basket resource in that you need natural materials and not
bought toys.

For instance, you will be able to collect many different types and size of
container, with and without lids. Cardboard or see-through tubes have many

uses. Safe lengths of metal chain, empty cones from knitting machine wool, old-fashioned wooden clothes pegs, large corks, big sponge hair curlers, large wooden curtain rings and other everyday and recycled natural materials.

You need to store the play materials in large cloth bags or similar containers that will keep the material dust-free and safe. You can bring out the materials once or twice a week as a special play time, so that the resource does not become over familiar.

You lay out the material attractively in a clear space and let toddlers play and explore as they wish. As with the Treasure Basket, the idea is that adults relax, look at and enjoy anything that toddlers wish to show them or with which they want help. Resist the temptation to direct the exploration or talk at the toddlers about what they are doing. Just follow their play with your eyes and ears and become no more involved than they ask of you.

Tidying up is part of the process, so warn the children in plenty of time and encourage them to participate in putting the materials back into the bags.

A safe, appropriate environment for physically active children

Babies and toddlers have a very strong drive to use their bodies, and to use all their skills in different ways and with a variety of objects.

- They need safe space for moving around, and the best area will often be on a comfortable floor.
- Do not be in a rush to get toddlers to sit up to a table for activities. Be prepared to play on the floor with them – enjoying the bricks, containers, sound-making toys or soft balls, or letting them crawl all over you.
- Follow the lead of babies and toddlers; they want to make things happen and to work out how their world works. So long as their environment is safe enough, you can let them learn from those objects they find fascinating now.
- Very young children need an environment that has enough interest but they do not need play materials chosen by adults whose main aim is to have something different out each session or day.

- Mobile babies and toddlers learn through a fair amount of repetition and by using similar actions on different materials. They need play materials that combine some happy familiarity with some novelty.
- Beware of being an over-busy adult; you can mainly let the children do the moving about. Sit close, show through your body language and words that you are available and they will show you what interests them.
- Be aware that boys and girls need similar levels of physical activity and excitement. There is much variation within the sexes and it is our adult expectations that make us surprised about 'lively' girls or 'timid' boys. Even from a young age, boys and girls can be directed unhelpfully towards patterns of behaviour, even if adults are not making fully conscious choices. Teams need to reflect on what they do and say in a constructive way.

 Adults learning from exploratory play

Elinor Goldschmied offered a very positive resource with her ideas for the Treasure Basket for babies and young toddlers, and the Heuristic Play session for young children. However, it is less helpful for children if these are seen as separate activities, with little reflection on how such an approach can inform the whole learning environment for young children.

Practitioners who have developed strong habits of intervention and imposing purpose on children's play can find sitting back to observe rather strange at first. Perhaps it is an insight into the experience of toddlers who find it so hard to stay still.

Consider the following and, if you work in a team, discuss them with colleagues.

- How far can the relaxed approach of watching and learning from very young children be extended into other parts of the day?
- What other sources of natural materials might there be that children could be enabled to experience?
- What can be learned from observing babies with the Treasure Basket, or toddlers with the Heuristic Play resources? Do I still have hidden assumptions about what is 'real play' and what is 'just messing about'?
- In what ways do/can I share the children's experiences of exploratory play with their parents?

6. Planning ahead for very young children

Coherence for learning within the early years

In England and Scotland the teams that developed the under-threes guidance materials chose not to call them a 'curriculum'. I think they were right because the word comes with too many 'school' associations. The idea of an early years curriculum is now well established for three- to five-year-olds. The different frameworks across the four nations of the UK have much in common, although the documents look different on the surface. At the time of writing (2006), Scotland and Northern Ireland continue respectively with 3–5 and 3–4 early years curricula. Wales is in the process of implementing a 3–7 years Foundation Phase and England is developing the 0–5 Early Years Foundation Stage. A 3–6 years Foundation Stage is under discussion in Northern Ireland.

Many of the problems have arisen because the early years have been defined as 'pre-school', rather than defining the school years as 'post-early childhood'. Without due care and attention paid to young children and their actual development, a curriculum for three- to five-year-olds can look far too much towards the beginning of formal schooling as a template for expectations and practice. There is good reason to be concerned about some practice with young children that has driven their learning through a narrow canyon of 'getting them ready for school'. Such a perspective creates even worse havoc if it presses on down to the under-threes – and sadly for children, where there is poor practice, that is exactly what has happened.

Developmentally appropriate, child-friendly practice – and there is much good quality in provision – is actively respectful of the unique aspects of helping babies and very young children as they learn. Babies are keen to explore but they apply their skills differently from four-year-olds. Toddlers are intrigued by how familiar objects can be sorted and organised. Yet they will not categorise or use words in the same way as three-year-olds. The cutting edge of learning for all children is at the boundary of what they understand now and what fascinates them at the moment.

A model from family life rather than school

It is striking how few books and articles draw on what works well in family life for the learning of very young children. The phrase, 'parents are their children's first teachers' is voiced much more often than any implication that these 'first teachers' have good ideas to which the 'second teachers' could well pay attention. I recently encountered the different phrase that 'parents are their children's first and continuing educators', and think this wording represents a better and more respectful view of parents.

Margaret Henry's book (1996) is one exception to this norm, and her discussion of the nature of early learning draws on the supportive nature of positive interactions in the family. Barbara Tizard (2002) especially through her practical research during the 1980s, made a constructive challenge to the assumptions that children's learning must be richer in early education settings or that a directive style of adult questioning necessarily helped children to learn.

Nurseries are not family homes but the best ones I have visited have a homely quality in which early years professionalism is viewed as totally compatible with close contact with children and respect for very ordinary activities of real meaning to babies and toddlers.

Many different ways of learning

Children learn through many different routes, of which play is one. However, an insistence that 'play is the vehicle for young children's learning' can create blocks for children's learning, especially for the youngest ones.

Learning from activities other than play

A kind of tunnel vision that claims children only learn through play can seriously underestimate how much children learn through happy involvement in daily routines, including their own care. Children's learning is best supported by a meaningful context that helps them to make connections, and they are greatly interested in playing their own part in daily life. There are many examples of what is meant by this within this book and the point is equally applicable to children older than three years. (For the ways in which caring routines can aid learning, see Chapter 3.)

Of course, children also learn through play activities and playful exchanges. However, it is important to avoid an over-emphasis on what will usually be understood as play. Otherwise, less experienced practitioners may focus exclusively on play materials rather than on what interests the children. Adults – parents as well as practitioners – are also then vulnerable to the marketing claims of manufacturers of toys, tapes, videos and other commercially produced materials which state that children's vital learning can only be supported through 'this play product'.

Routines

Young children do not want to be divided off from real daily life or be relegated to watching from the sidelines. They do not make any firm distinction between 'play' and what is enjoyable 'not play'. They are highly motivated to be part of what look to them like interesting adult activities. It is unwise in an early years setting or a family home to keep rigid distinctions between adult tasks and children's play.

- Look for safe ways to blur the boundaries for young children between play and daily routines. You can be guided by what they show they want to do and how they want to help. If toddlers find something interesting, they are far more likely to learn from the experience.
- Young children very much want to have a role within the domestic routine of the day. They like to feel trusted and of importance to you. Offer opportunities for this – see for instance the example of lunchtime on page 34, or taking messages on page 53.

- Look for all the opportunities for young children to be a part of what happens: tidying up, laying the table, fetching something for you, helping safely with a much younger child (by handing you something or making the baby smile), or watering the garden.
- It may seem easier to offer these opportunities in a family home, but nurseries can offer this kind of vital learning as well.
- Children will learn when you allow longer for such activities and value the time as a way to involve them. Young children will extend their skills of communication, practise their physical skills and feel a glow because they have helped. Keep an open mind – young children are often fascinated by everyday activities and daily routines that you may dismiss as rather boring.

Out and about

It is valuable to take babies and toddlers out and about in your local environment; the most ordinary of trips can be interesting to young children. Both they and you need to see a world outside the walls of a nursery or your home, and some young children have a long day with you. Children under two or three years old enjoy regular local circuits in which they start to recognise the last metres before you reach a landmark: the big tree, a fruit and vegetable market or the local library.

Toddlers are fascinated by events that seem ordinary to you because they are learning about how the world works. Posting letters, buying some bread or stopping to stare at a cat on a wall are of intense interest, and often of more value to very young children than organised special outings. Simple trips can be opportunities for young children to comment, recall and make choices.

Helping in the garden

Saplings Nursery has an outdoor area that is not as large as the gardens of some nurseries, but they have made the most of the possibilities and continue to reflect on how best to use the space. The toddlers have a separate outdoor time from the three- and four-year-olds. The babies have their own outdoor area that leads directly off their room.

During the morning of my visit, the toddlers (from about 18 months to 3 years) were busily engaged in many different activities. Two children were helping an adult with a hose: watering the plants in the large pots, hosing down one paved section and busily brushing and sweeping. Three more toddlers were absorbed in the earth area, digging and moving dirt about in a very concentrated way. This section of the garden also has some logs for sitting, and conversations took place here later. Other toddlers were busy on the fixed climbing equipment or running in energetic games. Apart from the adult holding the hose, other practitioners watched with clear interest and accepted invitations from children to join in any games.

Play needs to be playful for children

The over-emphasis on play as the crucial avenue for learning has led to a very high level of adult involvement in the planning, organising and interpretation of children's play experiences. Books and articles in the UK promote the advantages of 'play with a purpose', 'planning through play' and 'play as a medium for assessment and intervention'. Some of this material seems to lose the main plot of play as an activity in which children engage from choice, following their current interests and to their own ends. The children are at risk of becoming invisible, hidden by adult concern for all that play can be made to achieve. Some of the paper-heavy definitions of 'planning' have created a kind of harassment through so-called play when practitioners are anxious that their adult-led activity should 'deliver' on their pre-planned learning intentions. This approach is misguided for over-threes just as much as for much younger children.

Attentive adults, who are warm and playful companions, will notice the ways in which children choose to engage with play resources and adult-initiated experiences. Then it is possible to have a sound guess at what children have most likely learned from the experience and the short-term planning of a sensible 'what next?'

The best practice I have observed, within happy nursery rooms or in family homes, has been a relaxed following of the interests of babies and toddlers. The adults have an overall plan, informal in the case of families, of offering a range of activities, playful experiences, local outings and play materials over time. However, adult involvement or interested watching from close by, is informed by the key understanding that the cutting edge of young children's learning rests with their curiosity and wish to explore this item now.

The key factors in relaxed opportunities for young children to learn seem to be that early years practitioners:

■ use and trust their informal observation skills – alertness to what has caught the attention of young children means that adults can follow, rather than drive, the learning impetus, while attentive watching and listening also supports adult confidence that, of course, the children are learning, although perhaps in an unexpected direction

■ feel confident that following the children's lead of interest is not the same as losing control – adults remain responsible for setting boundaries, resolving disputes and keeping children safe.

The enthusiasm that needs to underpin young children's learning is focused on what has caught their attention for the moment. They need to feel emotionally connected by the desire to explore, to have enough challenge, but not too much, and to be able to experience satisfaction from the results of what they do.

Early years practitioners need to feel confident and supported by their seniors and managers. Alertness and the skills of observation enable engaged adults to be ready to join a child or to learn about that child by watching and listening. However, relaxed observation cannot support the day if practitioners are criticised by a manager who snaps 'Why aren't you doing anything?'. Any sense of pressure to look 'busy' will undermine the importance of watching, enjoying as well as literally doing something with children.

The learning process is more important than an end-product

Young children learn through self-chosen exploration or happily choosing from possibilities offered, but not insisted upon, by adults. Babies and toddlers want to experience interesting materials; their learning can be stunted if adults are tempted to drive the play with an art or craft product in mind. Young children may sometimes enjoy making a hand print, but often they will learn much more from their interest in feeling and scrunching paper or playing games with their hands and fingers. They learn from sensory experiences, and it is unwise for adults regularly to push toddlers and very young children towards an end-product.

Toddlers like hands-on activities, such as play dough, simple sticking and drawing. They relish the chance to feel, poke, push together and make something happen. Toddlers and two-year-olds often like to wield a paint brush, large crayon or chalk and make marks in whatever way they like. Young children like to feel materials and are thrilled by whole-body contact such as sitting in a paddling pool. Activities that give children pleasure and support their learning are often simple and physical.

I have heard other creative uses of the paddling pool from nurseries who have cooked up a batch of runny jelly or softly cooked pasta, filled the pool and let the toddlers splosh about in the material. Jelly and pasta feels squidgy, it runs through the fingers, can be pushed and made to flow and toddlers can just have a good time wallowing in it.

It is important for a team or individual childminder or nanny to reflect on any feelings that create pressure on very young children to produce something neat and attractive to adults. The value of arts and crafts activities can be badly undermined when you feel great pressure to ensure that a quality end-product emerges to be given to parents at the end of a nursery day. Babies and young toddlers do not make Easter cards and it is no use pretending that they do. If you feel you must have something to show at the end of the week you will be tempted to hold babies' feet to make a neat print or hold their hands to direct babies into sticking bits of paper or cotton wool onto the part of a card that you want. You may have the best of intentions, or feel it is the only way to show parents that you give children a valuable day, but there are others ways around this concern.

It is far better not to try to make something with babies and certainly not to build the week's planning around an end-product. You can offer enjoyable hands-on activities and take a photo of babies splashing and finger 'painting' in a flour and water mix. If you have a photographic record of an enthusiastic toddler painting, then it does not matter that he wants to layer on the paint so thickly that the paper in the end disintegrates.

It is also best to leave a toddler's work as close to the original as possible. You might mount it simply on card to help protect a painting or collage. In contrast, the work is no longer that of the toddler if you feel the need to cut round the painting, stick it on backing of your own making and add writing or other twiddly bits that the toddler cannot possibly have done.

Look also at good communication with parents to close the gap between what you have seen a child enjoy and a parent's question of 'what did he do today?' Parents do not always intend to put pressure on staff. They are genuinely interested to hear about their child's day, especially when a baby or toddler is unlikely to be able to tell them directly. Many parents will be thrilled by a photo and description, and they may well prefer this to cards that they can see were mainly finished by adults.

The scarf game at Saplings Nursery

When planning works well it is unobtrusive and practitioners feel confident to go with the flow of what has caught the attention of very young children. During my time in the baby room (up to 18 months), several mobile, young toddlers become intrigued with a collection of soft scarves.

■ Three of them started a game of holding onto a long scarf and half-walking, half-pulling each other in a line. Then they partially wrapped the scarf around themselves, then unwrapped and started once more. An adult continued to watch this game, ready to help if the toddlers became entangled at all. They only needed a brief moment of unravelling.

■ Another toddler took one scarf and sat on the floor, wrapping and unwrapping his truck in the scarf he had chosen. He looked utterly absorbed in ways to enclose his truck and was wrapping the scarf around, not simply covering the vehicle.

■ Two other toddlers experimented with covering each other's head with a scarf and then pulling it off. The turn-taking was accompanied by loud chortling.

■ One adult accepted an invitation from another child to play peek-a-boo and turns were taken over whether the scarf went over the child's or the adult's head.

The scarf game was developed by the toddlers themselves; at no point did the adults direct them at all. The adults watched and showed their interest and happiness that the toddlers were having a good time. It was clear to see that alert eyes were on the group that could potentially have become entangled in the long scarf. However, there was no 'watch out' or 'you might get hurt'. When invited, an adult joined in peek-a-boo as an equal partner. Each of the scarf games ended when one of the children wanted to finish.

Two ways to foot paint

I was struck by the difference in two anecdotes about foot painting with toddlers. A college tutor shared with me an activity that had made her deeply uneasy. A nursery team who felt they had to produce something had organised a foot-printing activity in which babies and toddlers were effectively moved down a conveyer belt of adults as their feet were used to print on paper.

In contrast, a nursery team described to me their recent successful foot-printing session. The toddlers were stripped down to their nappies, helped to step in the tray of paint and allowed to leave prints however they wanted on a long sheet of thick wallpaper. At the other end the toddlers went into a large container of water and paddled and splashed until the paint was gone.

Cleaning up had been part of the enjoyment.

 ## Genuine baby arts and crafts

A positive approach to young children's learning can help us to consider the balance between process (enjoying doing something and exploring) and a visible end-product. Toddlers and young children often relish arts and crafts activities, but in different ways from the slightly older children. Yet, they are often not ready to make something to show, and pressure on them spoils the activity and undermines their learning.

You could reflect on one activity, for example painting or working with play dough, and gather your ideas on how you can adjust the activity so it is appropriate for the younger children. In your experience:

- How do toddlers want to use the materials?
- How can you best handle any sense of pressure about having something to show, to parents or put on display, from very young children?
- How can practitioners share children's enjoyment and delight without relying on a print or card product made by children?

Planning for young children's learning

Good forward planning can support the learning of very young children so long as any tentative plans are grounded in knowledge of young children, attention to their skills and positive attitudes within the early years team.

All the considerations that are relevant when adults consider the play of slightly older children apply with even greater force when you observe valuable experiences for the learning of very young children.

- Practitioners and parents help children when they focus on the nature of early learning. Babies and toddlers add to their understanding and skills a bit at a time. They need to be enabled to make connections at their own pace. They learn when they are able to revisit play materials, games and locations (such as local outings) to enjoy the familiarity as much as explore some newness.
- Young children need to be able to practise, to repeat with slight variations what they enjoyed before and to take on novelty at their own rate. A level of repetition that would concern you in a four-year-old is developmentally appropriate for a toddler.
- Babies and toddlers absolutely need an experience of movement, not restriction, and they learn best through hands-on experience.
- They like repetition, for instance, with dropping or posting objects, because they find out for themselves if a similar action brings a similar result each time. They do not know the pattern of cause and effect for sure, so there is interest in discovery.

A range of materials, events and activities

Useful plans remain flexible and there should never be a sense of 'but it's on the schedule, we have to do it!' If toddlers have become interested in another activity or use of the materials, they will learn through following this source of exploration.

- A forward plan can cover your awareness of the full range of activities, play and routines that children can experience over the days and weeks. Some of these experiences arise from direct baby and child choice from an accessible indoor and outdoor learning environment – your planned, permanent provision.
- A guiding plan for the week, or a two- to three-week cycle, is a good way to time in a range of adult-initiated experiences (I call them the 'specials') that can be offered to children; and they can then genuinely choose to take advantage of the very open-ended simple art activity or cooking – or choose not to get involved hands-on today. Young children

cannot ask to do something 'again' until they have experienced it for the first time – so, of course there is a place for experiences offered by flexible early years practitioners.

■ Interesting events like a rainbow, heavy rain, the window cleaner, anything of interest to the children, take precedence over the working plan for the morning. Dry or warmer weather after a spell of grey wetness is a sign to get out on a local trip, no matter what the planning chart says.

■ Plans can give a possible time for activities like singing with young children who can enjoy a short group time with songs and hand rhymes that become more familiar. However, songs and music can happen throughout the day; there should be no sense of 'But we sing at 3.00, not now'. If children want a song, now is the time to sing it.

■ Very young children have difficulty with a group story time; they need a book when they request it and to sit close, probably in your lap or with no more than a 'sofa-full', either on a sofa or in a comfy, snuggling-in area indoors or out.

Flexible use of the environment

All settings have to deal with the available space, and spaces, of their building. Some have to resolve the potential difficulties of small rooms; other settings need to make friendly corners and areas out of a large open space.

■ A useful learning environment makes the best possible use of space and has accessible resources stored so that children can make their own choice, as well as help to put materials back when they have finished with them.

■ There may be special materials or a few items of equipment that adults bring out from time to time. Perhaps providing the Treasure Basket for babies or a Heuristic Play session for toddlers (see pages 66–68) happens regularly, but not every day. However, most materials can be available to children for their active choice; and the sense of exploratory play underpinning the Treasure Basket idea should be obvious within all play materials and activities.

■ Within the indoor and outdoor environments, you need space for babies and toddlers to move around. They need to move in their own way, without undue restriction.

- You can create areas that may focus on certain kinds of material but not in a rigid 'You play with that here' kind of organisation. Low furniture can be used to make helpful divisions, so that the toddlers looking at a book do not have to be wary of their friends pushing a little trolley.
- Useful equipment for baby and toddler rooms includes big cushions, comfortable floors and low, wall mirrors.
- Changing areas need to be hygienic but can still be welcoming, with pictures and photos on the wall, personal boxes for children and the removal of any cold, clinical feel to the room. Both you and the children will feel more comfortable in this room.

You can learn on the floor

Toddlers are happy sometimes to sit up at a table; they just do not want this to be the only way they are permitted to explore play materials. During my observations in many nurseries, it became clear how much young children prefer the environments in which they can move about and where adults are easily available at their eye level.

During my visit to Saplings Nursery, the staff responsible for the babies spent much of their time sitting on the floor or laying against large floor cushions. They stayed close by the non-mobile babies and were easily available to the mobile babies who came confidently to sit with adults, brought a book to share or simply leaned against an adult in a friendly fashion. Adults sit up to a low table for mealtimes and to support any arts and crafts activities. Mobile toddlers who want to do a painting or other hands-on activity can stand if they wish.

At Abacus Nursery, the practitioners in the baby room sit on the floor, close to the babies who are able to sit securely within an adult lap or use an adult as a hand hold or leaning aid.

At Staffordshire University Day Nursery, the baby room has a comfortable area with floor cushions and a low wall mirror. While I was there, one of the practitioners changed a baby's clothes (not his nappy) by the mirror. She took time to look, gently touch him and alert him to the image in the mirror. She then lay beside the alert baby, talking gently and touching him in full communication.

Choice and active choosing

Play materials need to be accessible for mobile babies and toddlers, so it is worth investing in low storage systems and simple containers that will hold different kinds of play materials.

An advantage of letting children choose is that tidying up becomes part of the play activity. If you have very limited space, then you may need to have a smaller selection of materials out for the children to play with at any one time, but still work to make it highly influenced by the children's choices.

Of course, tidying up after toddlers is hard work, but you can encourage their involvement and they will learn more by having been able to get access to a range of materials than by being very restricted in order to reduce the 'mess'.

Fixed equipment may usually be available, but even sand and water do not have to be available all the time. Different materials could be accessible on different days or parts of the day. On my visit to Abacus Nursery there was great excitement in the afternoon when a large container was brought out and many of the toddlers flocked around as they heard and recognised the sounds. The container had dry rice with play materials for handling it, and as soon as the container was stable on the floor toddlers started to feel and pour and shift the rice around.

 think

Children as part of planning

Very young children will not tell you in words how they feel about the different areas of the room and parts of the day. They will, however, show by their body language and behaviour what they enjoy the most, what is fun, what they tolerate and what is boring or provokes unhappiness. You can use observation skills to inform yourself about what very young children have probably learned and in what way today.

There are useful links to time spent with slightly older children, since there is always some unpredictability about how children will use play materials, activities and events. Potential or expected learning by the children is not usually exactly the same as what they *actually* learn when you watch

and listen closely. You can ask yourself and reflect with colleagues:

- In what ways did the babies and toddlers opt to use the activity?
- What did they probably learn and how close was this to what I anticipated?
- When I encourage children to make active choices, what directions do they take?
- How well do I let young children know what will happen a little in advance? Am I managing their expectations in a sensible way or am I sometimes moving too quickly without a wise level of prior warning?
- Do I listen to what children say in words and with their body language in order to hear how they reflect and comment on what they have done?

Useful play materials

Young children are very open-minded about what counts as interesting materials for play. This generation of very young children is targeted, through the adults who buy from shops and catalogues, with an unprecedented array of play materials. Some toys, kits and equipment are aggressively marketed as indispensable for children's healthy development and learning. However, the very young children of today are as ready as previous generations to be fascinated by large cardboard boxes, potatoes in the vegetable rack, saucepans, wooden spoons and any materials that are good to shake, touch and stack.

Unlike adults, young children are not influenced by how much something cost, the blurb on the box or other promotional material. On the contrary, they decide by whether something looks interesting and they can apply more than one or two actions to the materials. Young children are also very interested in everyday objects because they are used by, and so have meaning for, the adults and older children around them.

Ways to make music

One or two sound-making consoles may be fun for babies and toddlers but there is no point in buying half a dozen. There is a limit to what a young child can do when all the sound-making parts are fixed to a solid console. Babies and toddlers will learn more from a collection of separate sound-makers – many of which you can make – such as different materials sealed into see-through plastic bottles. Very young children can then explore one item at a time and act upon it in ways that they choose.

Babies and toddlers are very attuned to tone, rhythm, singing and music and much of their day can be tuneful. Some of the 'educational' material that has reached the UK from the United States promotes teaching very young children about Western classical composers, specifically Mozart. However, this focus is an unduly narrow approach to the enjoyment of music and is very culture-bound. Mozart wrote some fine music – do enjoy some of it with children – but there is no evidence that this specific kind of music boosts early development.

It is not helpful to have non-stop background music – be selective and use music in many appropriate ways with under-threes.

- Different types of music can be used as a gentle background for quieter times of the day or to mark a change in the routine.
- Toddlers and young children like music to dance to, either of their own accord or in the arms of adults. If you offer a choice of songs or instrumentals that are good for dancing, then children will start to show they recognise a tune and find ways to make requests.
- Children like to make music and are interested in any kind of music-maker.

Wise adult involvement

If young children are to learn from play, helpful adults need to reflect on how they get involved and how to avoid over-involvement that becomes interference.

- Enable young children to make choices by having materials easily available. Also be alert to how very young children express a choice. Babies may point with their eyes long before they are able to reach or point with a finger. They may make sounds of interest and approval, as well as disapproval and resistance.
- When you comment on children's choices do it in a way that shows you listen and look. You might say, even to a young baby, 'Oh, you'd like the teddy then?' or 'So you've had enough now?'
- When playing with babies be a willing participant in how the baby wants to explore, an equal playmate and not one who directs all the time. The adult should look spontaneous and unselfconscious, like the baby or toddler.
- Take turns and follow the child's lead in play just as often, if not more, than you make a suggestion by words or actions.
- Children themselves decide when an activity is at an end or if there is more mileage in it. Young children are irritated if they are stopped prematurely, especially if there has been no warning about 'tidying up soon'. Also, they will stop learning when their interest has faded and, even if you manage to make them stay at the activity, the child's mind will have gone somewhere more interesting.

- Enable and encourage young children to play together by making materials easily available, so that the children can organise their own game with the hats from the dressing-up materials or building an enclosure with the bricks.
- Watch from a friendly distance, so you are able to communicate your interest and intervene only if necessary.
- Be close enough to accept any invitation to join the game but create a friendly distance so that you are not on top of children all the time.

Fishes on the cushion

In Saplings Nursery, a number of two-year-olds showed interest in a container with different-sized toy fish. An adult stretched out on the floor beside the children and helped them put out fishes of their choice on a large floor cushion. The practitioner showed by her actions that the name of each kind of fish was written underneath it. The young children themselves expressed intrigue in the different sizes of fish, in whether or not they had teeth, and in the shark-type fish that snap at others. The adult followed the children's interest and the exploration finished when the children had had enough.

Playing pretend zoos

In Staffordshire University Day Nursery, the two- and three-year-olds were playing in the garden. There was a long and happy sequence in which several children were in a large pull-along trolley. An adult was pulling and another child pushing from behind.

The children were playing 'going to the zoo' and various parts of the garden had imaginary animals, chosen mainly by the children and then 'seen', talked about and sometimes shrieked at. Other members of staff also in the garden sometimes became one of the animals, including some of the scarier ones like a crocodile or snake.

The game lasted for many different animals and several circuits of the garden and stopped when the children had had enough.

A child's eye view of social skills

We need to recognise the social skills that children are learning along with all their other skills. Life for young children with other under-threes is not always plain sailing. Adults need to help negotiation and problem-resolution in a way that leaves children more able to resolve the situation next time.

Watch carefully how the young children in your setting need to use social skills. Many adults tend to focus on 'sharing' as important. The different skills that make up what adults mean by 'sharing' are more complex for children than we often allow. Look for opportunities when you can ease the situation, for instance if a child:

- looks as if he wants to join a group whose game is already well-established
- wants to suggest and lead, but finds it hard not to come across as 'bossy'
- seems to be over-organised by other children and finds it hard to say 'No', for example she does not appear to want to be the baby every time in the home corner play
- wants very much to build his own tower and another child keeps trying to help.

Of course, it is not always easy to be a helpful adult, but an important first step is to tune into children and recognise the social skills they are learning.

Learning abstract concepts

A serious problem arising from the pressures on early years practitioners is the temptation to try to get very young children to learn abstract ideas. The difficulties arise for several interrelated reasons, most of which highlight the need for adults to look through children's eyes and hear with their ears.

Ideas that seem obvious to adults, because they have lived with them for so long, are far from obvious to young children. The main point about this area of learning is that colour, shape, number, size and all the other abstract concepts are ways of describing the world; they do not exist in their own right. You cannot see a 'red', lift a 'heavy' or do a 'fast'. You see a pair of trousers that are red, try to lift a heavy box, or have fun running fast with your friends.

These words are a way of describing, of pinning down, the characteristics of objects, actions and the environment as it is experienced. They are neither objects nor actions and so do not relate to the language of a young child who deals mainly in 'naming and doing words' – the most useful vocabulary when you are a young language learner.

So, well-intentioned adults who start asking toddlers 'what colour is this car?' or 'how many bricks have we got?' are often met with incomprehension; the question makes no sense. Some children deal with the confusion with silence, a useful ploy if an adult is talking 'nonsense' but seems to be serious about it, rather than having a joke. Cooperative young children try to answer by echoing what sounds like the key word or confidently answering 'colour', as if they think perhaps this is an alternative name for what most people have so far called a 'car'.

Young children learn about abstract concepts through a considerable amount of varied experience and hands-on exploration of their world. Practitioners and parents can be a genuine help in many ways, most of which mean avoiding the sense of pressure to make this learning happen now rather than later. If you relax and listen to children, you will also gain fascinating insights about how they are beginning to make sense of their world in terms of the qualities of objects, how to compare and contrast, and in what ways things can be the 'same' or 'different'.

Adults need to hold a full, rich understanding of all the abstract concepts that children will learn over the first five or six years of their life. A narrow view seems to have developed that only colour and shape are really important. Confusion for practitioners, and parents, can arise because these concepts are heavily pushed in some topic books. Colour and shape, often along with written letters and numbers, are frequently made an integral part of many plastic toys and so-called 'early learning' pads and tables. The more narrow practice approaches that I observe tend to home in on 'colour of the week' and lots of practice in being able to know circles, squares and similar two-dimensional shapes.

In fact young children learn step by step about much more than colour and shape. Colour, in particular, can be a tough idea for children to grasp, until they home in on this particular characteristic of an object. Other concepts can be experienced more directly through physical actions, and are often understood far earlier. Helpful adults need to watch and listen for any of the early steps into abstract concepts and not behave as if some kinds of conceptual thinking are more valuable than others. You want to encourage this development of thinking and it does not matter which concepts emerge first. It does matter that young children feel adults share their interest in recognising and exploring this difference.

You will also find that detailed observation of young children will highlight that individuals become interested in rather different ideas.

- Young children may begin to understand weight and relative weight through lifting, pushing and manipulating materials of different weights.
- Height is often of interest, but not necessarily height of people. Keen climbing toddlers may take on board the idea of 'too high' in contrast to heights that adults are happy for them to scale or jump down from.
- Speed is often a matter of great interest, probably initially on the fast rather than the slow side. Children watch fast vehicles or like to run fast and chase each other.
- Temperature, especially a wariness about 'hot', can be a practical part of adult safety warnings to young children. Some concepts are composed of opposites and gradations in between. So children may come to realise that hot is the opposite end of cold, and warm is somewhere in between.
- Texture is interesting because of the contrast between soft and gentle textures that are pleasant to touch and rub, and the more rough surfaces that can hurt.
- Sound may be important in terms of enjoyable volume, 'too loud' (especially for children who do not like very loud or sudden noises), or soft whispering that can be fun.
- Some children are especially interested in 'broken' and learn that some things can be put back together and so are not really broken, some things can be mended and some things are broken forever.

When young children become genuinely interested in colour, those colours that first catch their attention and make meaning for them will probably be objects that matter in their world. Perhaps Tom has a favourite green bike that he always wants to ride at playgroup, Farjana has a lovely soft blue pair of trousers and Anneka knows the yellow dump truck on the cover of the best book in the nursery.

Children think about aspects of the world that matter to them or happen to puzzle them; it is a very individual development. The focus for their first abstract concepts will be through what has meaning for them; you need to know the child. For instance, by two and a half years my daughter Tanith had an important concept about what she called 'pokey things'. This phrase was applied to plants and bushes with sharp leaves or thorns and was significant to her because of our family habit of going for country walks. This enabled her to explain why she was unhappy emerging from the undergrowth, having been scraped by the pokey things and why she definitely needed to be carried now.

In order to make sense of any abstract concept, young children have to experience the idea in action.

- They need to be able to feel textures, manipulate different weights, see the difference between 'light on' and 'light off' or the 'dark' winter evening, when it is possible to see the moon on the walk home.
- Young children do not need a 'colour of the week' or a 'shape table'. They will learn steadily if they are interested in visually matching and sorting different basic colours, or posting and sorting shapes. Adults can help by low-key conversation and by avoiding any testing questions like 'What shape is this?'
- Provide the concept words as part of your natural conversation. You can say, 'Oh, feel this blanket. It's so lovely and soft' or 'What a loud noise, that made me jump'.
- You can talk about what you are handling or trying to find with 'I need a bigger wedge here' or 'Where did I put that blue cup? I saw it a moment ago'.
- You can help children to notice by showing them direct comparisons that do not put them on the spot, for instance, 'I think we need another square shape now; we need another one like this' (showing the child).
- You can also help a child extend their language. For instance, 'Yes your Daddy is big isn't he? He is really tall. I think he's even taller than Matt from the baby room. Shall we ask them to measure against each other?'

In this way children will learn the words and the context in which to apply them, and their confusion will be much reduced.

Looking for the first abstract concepts

Observation skills are once again a tremendous support for tuning into children as a helpful adult. Toddlers often show evidence of the development of abstract concepts as they approach their second birthday, but they may not be recognised as such.

I reread the list I made of my daughter's spoken vocabulary when she had just turned two years old. Along with many naming and doing words and a variety of short phrases, Tanith also used a range of words to describe important aspects to her world. These included:

- the words 'hot', 'warm' and 'cold', the modifier of 'bit warm' and applications like 'nose bit cold'
- the words 'crunchy' and 'tasty', which were applied to food
- comments on sound such as 'squeaky', 'noisy' and 'big bang'
- words that showed an awareness of light, most particularly the situation when the light was switched off, for example 'very dark'
- words linking fact and fantasy – for example she would make a joke by saying something everyone knew was untrue, then laugh and say 'Just teasing' or 'Just pretend'.

Other children would not show anything like an identical pattern. It will depend on what interests them. My son was more interested at this age in height, linked with his keenness for climbing and walking along local walls. He made his own decisions often about 'too high wall'. He also expressed the difference between 'old' and 'new', and applied then to the holes he went through in the churchyard hedge during his evening walks with his father. 'Old hole' already existed and 'new hole' had, I think, been created by vigorous shoving.

- Why not look and listen to the toddlers and young two-year-olds in your care?
- For the time being, ignore the concepts of colour or shape. Young children are interested in, and are learning about, many other concepts. In what ways can you hear them describe the differences in their personal world?

7. Building blocks for good practice

The current expansion of childcare for very young children has focused attention onto what makes a positive experience for babies and toddlers, as well as aspects of poor practice that should be avoided.

Research over the last few decades has highlighted that the development of very young children is promoted through affectionate and personal exchanges between caring adults and children. Babies and toddlers need attention that is adjusted to their temperament, interests and current pattern of learning. Meanwhile adults remain as central to young children as ever. Children need their care and carers to:

■ notice and respond to their individual needs, concerns and interests – young children need a secure base of one or two people to whom they feel confident to return

■ be sensitive to the uniqueness of a child's communication and keen to tune into an individual baby or toddler

■ be consistent between a small number of adults.

Caring for and attention to a child's physical needs is part of this individual approach. Consequently, quality can never be achieved within services for the very early years if care is undervalued. People who marginalise care are marginalising the young children themselves.

Babies and young children are primed and ready to learn, in their own way and at their own pace. Early learning happens throughout the day, and in any setting, whether group or home-based care, that is organised and committed to children's learning. It is a substantial misunderstanding to restrict 'early learning' to particular kinds of setting or claim it can only be delivered by particular kinds of early years practitioners. Children will benefit from a well-trained early years workforce who are open to continued professional development and to reflection within teams and with colleagues.

Children are enabled to learn step by step when we adults consider our role in a positive and reflective way.

- We need to use our observation skills to learn, tune into and admire what babies and children can do now and what they can nearly manage.
- We need to see them as young and small individuals who can do many things, rather than focus on the long list of what they do not yet know or skills they cannot yet manage.
- Very young children are ready to be enthusiastic; they do not need to be motivated to learn. However, they can be diverted away from this enthusiasm. If adults are unpredictable and harsh, young children's energy is redirected into dealing with a world that is unpleasant and uncertain. If adults are over-directing, even the more resilient children risk becoming passive and choosing not to exercise choice.
- On the other hand, attentive and interested adults go with the flow of the interest of very young children, and encourage their enthusiasm for learning and for persevering even if something is hard at the outset.
- Children are in the learning business for the long haul. What is done well with very young children can help point them towards emotional well-being, a sense of self-worth and a keenness to discover. All of these positive dispositions are needed by children as they pass through the later years of childhood.
- We need to focus on what and how young children can learn now. We need to resist any pressure to push them onwards to skills or ideas that somebody claims are more important and valuable. Many skills and scaffolds of knowledge cannot work properly without the foundations.
- Lessons from brain research, as well as the observations of experienced practitioners, are that trying to fast track children is far more likely to knock them off the track. Worse still, bullying children in this way can create such negative attitudes towards themselves and learning that they will not want to get back on track again.

Combining good quality care with learning for very young children is not technically difficult. However, it does need emotional as well as physical energy, an intellectual interest in how babies and toddlers learn, and a passion for relishing the moments. I have learned a great deal through consultation and training with a range of early years practitioners. Sharing ideas and experiences has confirmed my personal observations that what makes a good day and positive relationships for very young children has a very great deal in common with what makes a good day for slightly older children.

I have always been resistant to calling young children 'pre-schoolers', because this label defines them in terms of the next social experience, with the risk that their learning is seen only as the precursor to school, not as significant in its own right. We do not, for instance, call teenagers 'pre-workers', and need to focus on young children as they are now, not 'pre-' anything.

The more I learn about under-threes the more strongly I feel about approaching and valuing them as individuals in their own right: incredibly interesting, very tiring to be with on occasion and a source of fascinating insights on how to act upon the world and what everyday events mean. Babies and toddlers come afresh to each day, ready to be amazed and get seriously stuck into experiences. The task of adults, practitioners or parents, is very much more satisfying if we let some of that freshness rub off on us.

Resources

National guidance and developments

Guidance materials are usually free for practitioners working within the country of issue. Otherwise you may need to purchase anything that cannot be downloaded from the website.

Birth to Three Matters: A framework to support children in their earliest years. Prolog: 0845 6022 260. Research review can be downloaded from the CD-ROM or purchased as a booklet (RR444), summary free from Prolog (RB444) at *www.surestart.gov.uk/ensuringquality/birthtothreematters*

Birth to Three: Supporting our youngest children. Learning and Teaching Scotland: 0141 337 5000. *www.LTScotland.org.uk/earlyyearsmatters.* For the research review in summary go to *www.scotland.gov.uk/library5/social/ins6-00.asp* or for a full report *www.scotland.gov.uk/about/ED/IAC/00014478/page705680189.pdf*

For information about the Early Years Foundation Stage in England
Department for Education and Skills (2006) *The Early Years Foundation Stage: Consultation on a single quality framework for services for children from birth to five* download from *www.teachernet.gov.uk/publications*

Information about early years curriculum frameworks and current developments:

- The *Foundation Stage* in England *www.qca.org.uk*
- The *Foundation Phase* in Wales *www.learning.wales.gov.uk* or *www.accac.org.uk*
- The *Curriculum Framework for children 3–5* in Scotland
  www.ltscotland.org.uk/earlyyears/framechildren3to5.asp
- The *Curricular Guidance for Pre-School Education* in Northern Ireland and proposed Foundation Stage *www.deni.gov.uk/preschool/preschool_curricular.pdf*

General resources

Arnold, C (2003) *Observing Harry: Child development and learning 0–5.* Maidenhead: Open University Press.

Community Playthings (2005) *Creating Places: For birth to threes.* *www.communityplaythings.co.uk*

Dunn, J (1993) *Young Children's Close Relationships: Beyond attachment.* London: Sage.

Early Childhood Unit (2004) *Listening as a way of life* series. *www.ncb.org.uk/earlychildhood*

Edwards, A G (2002) *Relationships and Learning: Caring for children from birth to three.* London: National Children's Bureau.

Elfer, P, Goldschmied, E and Selleck, D (2003) *Key Persons in the Nursery: Building relationships for quality provision.* London: David Fulton Publishers.

Goddard Blythe, S (2004) *The Well Balanced Child: Movement and early learning.* Stroud: Hawthorn Press.

Goldschmied, E and Jackson, S (2004) *People under Three: Young children in day care.* London: Routledge.

Goldschmied, E and Selleck, D (1996) *Communication Between Babies in their First Year,* book and video. London: National Children's Bureau.

Gopnik, A, Meltzoff, A and Kuhl, P (1999) *How Babies Think: The science of childhood.* London: Weidenfeld & Nicholson.

Healy, J (2004) *Your Child's Growing Mind: A practical guide to brain development and learning from birth to adolescence.* US: Main Street Books.

Henry, M (1996) *Young Children, Parents and Professionals: Enhancing the links in early childhood.* London: Routledge.

Hughes, A M (2006) *Developing Play for the Under 3s: The Treasure Basket and Heuristic Play.* London: David Fulton Publishers.

Lindon, J (2005) *Understanding Child Development: Linking theory and practice.* London: Hodder Arnold.

Lindon, J (2003a) *Child Protection.* London: Hodder and Stoughton.

Lindon, J (2003b) *What Does it Mean to be Three?* and (2006) *What does it mean to be two?* Learnington Spa: Step Forward Publishing.

Lindon, J, Kelman, K and Sharp, A (2006) *Play and Learning with Under-threes.* London: Nursery World Books.

Ouvry, M (2000) *Exercising Muscles and Minds: Outdoor play and the early years curriculum.* London: National Early Years Network.

Penn, H (1999) *How Should we Care for Babies and Toddlers?* Childcare Research and Resources Centre, University of Toronto *www.childcarecanada.org/ resources/CRRUpubs*

Tizard, B and Hughes, M (2002) *Young Children Learning: Talking and thinking at home and at school.* Oxford: Blackwell.

Videos/DVDs

Baby it's You. Beckmann Visual Publishing: 01624 816585 *www.beckmanndirect.com*

Infants at Work: Babies of 6–9 months exploring everyday objects and *Heuristic Play with Objects: Children of 12–20 months exploring everyday objects.* National Children's Bureau: 020 7843 6029 *www.ncb.org.uk*

Tuning into Children. Book and video from National Children's Bureau.

The High/Scope Approach for Under Threes. High/Scope UK: 020 8676 0220 *www.high-scope.org.uk*

Attachment in Practice and other titles. Siren Film and Video Ltd: 0191 232 7900 *www.sirenfilms.co.uk*

The Social Baby and *The Social Toddler.* The Children's Project: 020 8546 8750 *www.childrensproject.co.uk*

Learning Together with Babies and *Learning Together with Ones* (Twos, Threes and Fours). PEEP Centre: 01865 779779 *www.peep.org.uk*

Key Times: A framework for developing high quality provision for children under three years old. A video and pack on good practice developed by Camden EYDCP, 2006. Open University.

Index